Praise for *Made for More*

Hannah Anderson's book *Made for More* is refreshing. It locates the real discussion of what a "woman's role" is or isn't in both men and women being made in the image of God and tasked with the care of creation. This challenges the self-absorbed literature regarding women that has become the norm, as well as self-satisfied women who are content to do little for the kingdom.

KATHY KELLER, New York City

One of the biggest questions dividing the church today is "What counts as biblical femininity?" In *Made for More*, Hannah Anderson reminds us of the more fundamental question: "What counts as biblical humanity?" This personal, lyrical, and deeply theological meditation invites us to the common ground so often forgotten in our disputes and offers a gospel vision of *imago dei* regained through union with Christ. While directed to women, it is not simply a "women's book" focused on the "pink" passages but a rich portrait of the "more" that God has for all of us as He conforms us to the Image of His Son.

DEREK RISHMAWY, director of college and young adult ministries, Trinity United Presbyterian Church, Santa Ana, CA

I have sometimes thought that the emphasis on gender roles was an understandable response to their erosion within the broader culture. Hannah Anderson has a message with the same goal, but a different strategy: Here is a book for women that has something to teach men beyond what women want or talk about when we are not around. By pointing our attention toward the massive backdrop of the image of God, Anderson isn't trying to downplay or ignore differences between the sexes but rather to let them emerge naturally as both sexes ground their lives in the love of God. This is a wise, clear, and well-written book that I heartily commend to everyone made in the image of God, male and female alike.

MATTHEW L. ANDERSON, lead writer at mereorthodoxy.com and author of *The End of Our Exploring*

Here at last is a book about Christian womanhood that I can read and recommend, a book that builds a biblical view of womanhood not with proof texts but with foundational doctrines, a book that draws not upon trendy bestsellers but upon the greatest thinkers and writers in history. *Made for More* transcends narrow, contemporary gender debates with a clear and compelling call for all of us to flourish as human beings made in the image of God.

KAREN SWALLOW PRIOR, author of *Booked: Literature in the Soul of Me* and *Fierce Convictions: The Extraordinary Life of Hannah More—Poet, Reformer, Abolitionist*

Can women "have it all"? In *Made for More*, Hannah Anderson reminds us that debating whether women can have fulfilling families and careers isn't the right place to begin in answering that question. Instead, she argues that women do have it all: we are full image-bearers of a great and glorious God. As Anderson unpacks the truth of what it means to be fully human and created in God's likeness, she skirts the trendy controversies of the day, instead offering women a strong scriptural foundation for understanding our identity. While the mommy wars rage, Anderson's still, small, and eloquent voice calls women to a deeper, freeing vision of all that God intended womanhood to be.

AMY LEPINE PETERSON, mother, TESOL instructor, and freelance writer

This is a book about human flourishing, directed at humans who also happen to be women. Hannah Anderson wants us to understand that, from the cradle to the grave, women are image-bearers of God. Grasping the significance of being made *Imago Dei* changes the way we relate to God, to others, and to creation. It changes the way that we think about relationships, education, work and success. And it makes developing and employing our gifts imperative instead of optional. Hannah asks women to broaden their gaze, to look beyond the "pink passages" of Scripture to the full counsel of God's Word, to understand that our ultimate purpose is not to be like Esther or Ruth but like Christ himself. Any discussion of identity must start with this recognition. This book is a needful reminder that all of us, men and women alike, are created to uniquely bear the image of our Maker "from life's first cry to final breath."

JEN WILKIN, Bible teacher and author of *Women of the Word: How to Study the Bible with Both Our Hearts and Our Minds*

To find and understand yourself, you must find and understand God first. That is the simple yet vastly profound message of this book. In other words: If you have ever been restless, if you have ever been disappointed or confused about your life, if you have ever wondered how to discover the "more" that something in you longs for—this is a book for you to savor. Don't be surprised if you pause often to let the sentences sink in deeply. That is where sentences like these belong.

LISA VELTHOUSE, author and collaborator on five books, founding editor of PickYourPortion.com

In an age where women are looking for "more," Hannah Anderson gives us the only addition that will not be taken away: life as an eternal soul in the image of God. Her writing is clear and her perspective hopeful. Today's women, especially the younger generation, are burdened with doubt and cynicism about who they are and why they are here. Anderson writes with assurance and grounded optimism. We need her fresh voice in this generation. I highly recommend it!

LUMA SIMMS, author of *Gospel Amnesia: Forgetting the Goodness of the News* and *Counterfeit Me*

We have all played a role shifting, justifying, and sidestepping in pace with our culture. Hunting for a deeper peace, a stronger anchor, and a steadier foot, Hannah's words bring truth back to center—where God is the North Star of our souls. Hannah uses her gift of contemplation to be the gentle hand lifting the faces of her sisters to gaze upon the strength and beauty of that Star.

CHRISTI ZIEBARTH, artist and educator

Made for More is a warm conversation about humanity, life, and value, and the journey that each of us must take in coming to grips with God and ourselves. From the first pages, Hannah offers hope, safety, and even joy by reminding us of who we are as people made in God's image. No matter where you are in your journey, *Made for More* invites you to a life of health and wholeness for today, tomorrow, and into eternity. We will use this book often as we disciple women in homes, churches, chapels, and Bible studies.

CHRIS AND KELLY WALLACE, US Army

As a counselor, mentor, and parent, I am compelled to assist others to understand why we were made and what we are made to do. Salvation is the beginning of a lifelong pursuit of our place in God's creation. *Made for More* challenges each Christian to passionately endeavor to reflect God within their unique sphere of influence.

DELDEE MCCALEB HINDMAN, wife, mother, mentor/counselor

I've read many books on womanhood and am pleased Hannah Anderson has written a book that finally gets underneath the issue and addresses the necessity of understanding personhood. Hannah graciously rises above the gender debates and will challenge you out of every "category" you think you are in and place you in the only one that matters . . . in the image of Christ. This is a beautifully written book useful for women looking to deepen their understanding of their Creator as well as how they are to live and love like Jesus.

SUZIE B. LIND, pastor of women's ministry, King's Harbor Church. Torrance, California

Drawing our eyes back to our Maker, again and again, Hannah Anderson teases out the beauty of being *made*, a created being, for creative purposes, in the image of God. Using rich images and deep theology, she pliably molds the *gender* issue into a *human* issue—one that should concern every one of us in profound ways.

LORE FERGUSON, blogger, speaker

MADE *for* MORE

An Invitation to Live in God's Image

HANNAH ANDERSON

MOODY PUBLISHERS

CHICAGO

All Scripture quotations, unless otherwise indicated, are taken from *The Holy Bible,
English Standard Version.* Copyright © 2000, 2001 by Crossway Bibles, a division of Good
News Publishers. Used by permission. All rights reserved.

Scripture quotations marked NIV are taken from the Holy Bible, New International Ver-
sion®, NIV®. Copyright © 1973, 1978, 1984, 2011 by Biblica, Inc.™ Used by permission
of Zondervan. All rights reserved worldwide. www.zondervan.com. The "NIV" and "New
International Version" are trademarks registered in the United States Patent and Trademark
Office by Biblica, Inc.™

Scripture quotations marked KJV are taken from the King James Version.

All emphasis shown in Scripture quotations have been placed by the author.

Edited by Pam Pugh
Interior design: Erik M. Peterson
Page composition: Smartt Guys design
Author photo: Mary Wall
Cover design: Faceout Studio
Cover images: Shutterstock # 90914738 / #11091787

Library of Congress Cataloging-in-Publication Data

Anderson, Hannah, 1979-
  Made for more : an invitation to live Imago Dei / Hannah Anderson.
     pages cm
  Includes bibliographical references.
  ISBN 978-0-8024-1032-0
  1. Theological anthropology--Christianity. 2. Image of God. 3. Christian life. I. Title.
  BT701.3.A53 2014
  233'.5--dc23

                          2013039480

We hope you enjoy this book from Moody Publishers. Our goal is to provide
high-quality, thought-provoking books and products that connect truth to your real
needs and challenges. For more information on other books and products written and
produced from a biblical perspective, go to www.moodypublishers.com or write to:

Moody Publishers
820 N. LaSalle Boulevard
Chicago, IL 60610

3 5 7 9 10 8 6 4 2

Printed in the United States of America

To Nathan,
who holds my hand
as we walk this road to glory.

Contents

Acknowledgments

One of the first things that you learn about being an image bearer is that none of us bear His Image alone. Our existence is one of union and communion, of shared stories and intersecting lives. I'm grateful to God for sovereignly placing these other image bearers in mine—apart from them I couldn't do the work I do or be the woman He has created me to be.

For Nathan who willingly embraces this crazy, philosophical woman and is content with burnt pancakes because there are simply too many other things to think about.

For Phoebe, Harry, and Peter whose existence daily reaffirms my belief in a creative, life-giving God.

For Eden whose friendship has challenged (and provoked) me for over 15 years. Here, dear one, all our conversations have finally made it to print.

For the Moody Team for taking a risk on a no-name writer with nothing more than a big idea.

For all my blog readers (particularly my mother and aunts) who faithfully "liked" and forwarded my writing. This is nepotism at its finest.

For the communion of saints—past, present, and future—who have invested their lives in my spiritual formation, whether it was Sunday School, overnight camping trips, prayer meetings, or choir practice. Thank you.

Getting Started

"For from Him and through Him and to Him are all things." —Romans 11:36

One of the difficulties of writing a book is defining your audience.

While we authors love to think that our work will smash through barriers, top all the lists, appeal to readers young and old, male and female alike—that we will finally achieve literary perfection in one, single-bound volume—our publishers know better. This book is written primarily to women (although biased as I am, I believe that it could be beneficial to men as well).

Normally, this isn't an issue of any interest, but in this case, it is divinely ironic. The irony comes because the goal of this book is to call women to recover an understanding of ourselves that is more basic than our gender. It's a call to recover the image of God in our lives—to re-imagine not simply what it means to be a woman but what it means to be a person *made in the very likeness of God Himself.*

Ours is a culture defined by categories. And in recent years, it seems that more and more of us actually think of ourselves (and others) in these ways *first*—we are men or women; we are black, white, Hispanic, or other; we are Libertarians or Democrats; and we are low-income or part of the elite 1 percent.

The only thing we no longer are is simply human.

This need to identify ourselves by categories invades the church as well. Often we shape entire ministries around our distinctives, separating ourselves by age, theology, and style of worship. Sometimes this is necessary in response to specific issues—in answer to our culture's gender ambiguity for example, we have diligently guarded biblical norms and have encouraged men and women to pursue masculinity and femininity. But I'm afraid something has happened in the process. I'm afraid we've developed a touch of identity myopia.

As our categories—our race, our gender, our calling—have become central to how we understand ourselves, as they have become the *only* things that we can see clearly, we have developed a nearsightedness of the soul. We can see the details well enough, but we can't grasp their significance; and when we glance away from them, even momentarily, everything else is out of focus and blurred. As a result, we can't understand ourselves, other people, or even God Himself.

We need to recover a vision for the big picture. We need to be able to see the things that are at a distance. To understand that we are defined, not by our categories, but by being made in the image of God and that our ultimate identity is to reflect and represent Him on this earth. To know that everything about life—from our gifting to our gender to our personality—flows *"from Him and through Him and to Him,"* that our very existence is linked deeply and inextricably to His.

Because when you understand this, when His identity becomes the foundation for your identity, the details will finally make sense. You will finally be able to see them for what they are. You will finally understand that they are not ends in themselves, but means to an end—the greater end of reflecting God's nature and representing Him on this earth. The greater end of becoming like Him.

This book is not a call to deny womanhood in order to embrace being made in His image. But it is a call to understand that womanhood, and everything that comes with it, serves a greater purpose. It is not a call to abandon labels or categories, but it is a call to step back in order to lay a solid foundation before we build those categories. It is a call to wrestle with what it means to be made in His image and to believe that you are made for more than what you often settle for.

And ultimately, it is a call—no, an *invitation*—to re-imagine yourself, not simply as a woman, but first and foremost as a person destined to be like your God.

part one | *From Him . . .*

We've tried to answer how identity manifests itself without first answering where identity comes from. We've tried to figure out where a woman should spend her life without first answering who she should be.

In order to know who you are, you must first know who He is.

chapter 1

Who Am I?
Courage to Question,
Faith to Find the Answer

"We have all forgotten what we really are."
—*G. K. Chesterton*

After being homeschooled for two years, my seven-year-old daughter entered second grade at our local elementary school.

Like any mom, I was an odd bundle of anxieties that first day. *Would she be scared? Would she make friends?* And perhaps more realistically, *Would she be so accustomed to homeschooling that she wouldn't be able to adapt and end would up being the "problem" child?* If I'm honest, I suppose I was mostly afraid that *I* would end up getting called to the principal's office to explain why my daughter expected to take a field trip once a week and thought that math class should involve baking.

But like most fears, mine ended up being largely unfounded and somewhat self-centered. Things went smoothly. Her first day was spent like anyone else's in getting to know the teacher, meeting her classmates, and establishing classroom rules and routines. Everything was flowing along nicely until her teacher turned to the class and asked, "Does anyone have any questions?"

Immediately my Phoebe's hand shot up.

"I have a question," she responded with all seriousness. "Why are we here? I mean, why are we like this? Why do we have hands and why do we sit in desks and why do we go to school? Why do we have feet? And why do we have to listen? Why are we made this way? *Why?* I just want to know, *Why*?!"

So much for keeping a low profile as the new kid.

When my friends heard about it as was inevitable in our small town, there were a lot of teasing comments with most of them to the effect of "like mother, like daughter." And while it is true that she comes by her philosophical disposition honestly, I think I would have found it funnier if her questions hadn't hit so close to home. Her questions—her need to understand herself and her place in this world—are the very same questions that each of us wants to have answered too. Despite being grown adults, how many of us wish we could just raise our hand like a little girl on the first day of school and ask, "Who am I and why am I here?"

Searching for Ourselves

This need to understand ourselves, to wrestle with who we are and where we fit in the world, is fundamentally a search for identity. It is a journey to discover, not some foreign land or distant galaxy, but a world much closer—one whose very proximity can make it all the more mysterious, profound, and quite frankly, dangerous. It is a search, not simply to discover what it means to be a woman, but more important: what it means to be a person, what it means to be *you*.

But because this search can be unsettling, we tend to avoid it the same way we avoid looking full-faced into the mirror. Instead of wrestling with the deeper questions of life, we distract ourselves and find identity in things like relationships, jobs, political causes, or hobbies. We check boxes, make lists, and categorize ourselves by race, religion, and socioeconomic status. We calculate our bodies in pounds, inches, and clothing sizes, all in an effort to gain the security that comes from knowing exactly who we are and where we fit into the grand scheme of things. After all, if I know that I am a married, blonde-haired, blue-eyed, extroverted, mother of three who studied liberal arts, writes, likes to travel, watches classic movies, and enjoys long walks on the beach, then certainly I must know who I am, right? *Right?*

Unfortunately, while roles and categories provide us some measure of stability in an uncertain world, the problem comes when these things change, as they inevitably do. The loss of a job, a broken marriage, unexpected illness, infertility, or churches that fail us. And suddenly the questions we had succeeded in repressing flood back to the surface. For Phoebe, it was something as simple as transitioning from home to school—suddenly her world shifted and she found herself needing to affirm the most basic realities of her life.

Perhaps even more surprisingly, good times can initiate the search for identity as often as bad. When we finally get that new job or finish that graduate degree; when we meet that someone we've been waiting to spend the rest of our life with; when the babies come and we're able to nurture our hopes and dreams with them. Even in these moments, as we come down from the emotional high, we realize that they didn't fulfill us the way we had expected; despite having invested so much of ourselves in what we thought would provide a lasting sense of meaning, we hardly know ourselves in the midst of it. We begin to feel detached and distant, outsiders looking in on our own lives. And the things that we once looked to for stability and identity begin to feel like burdens and obligations instead of blessings.

Just ask Elizabeth Gilbert.

By anyone's standard's, Elizabeth's life was a success; she had graduated from the best schools, had a terrific career that took her around the world, and together with her husband owned an impressive home in New York's Hudson Valley. And yet, she spent most nights crying herself to sleep only to awaken with the persistent awareness that little about her life made sense. She felt overwhelmed by duty and directionless about her future. So at a young thirty-two, she checked out. She divorced her husband, threw herself into a dysfunctional relationship, and eventually quit her job to travel the world. Her journey took her through Italy and India and all the way to Indonesia; she sampled *la dolce vita* in Rome and Tuscany and committed herself to religious asceticism in a Hindu ashram—all in an attempt to find some sense of personal stability, some sense of lasting identity.

Elizabeth shared her journey in a memoir she called simply *Eat, Pray, Love*. Within weeks, it hit the top of the *New York Times* bestseller list, popped up in book clubs everywhere, and went on to sell over ten million copies. And that's when it became startlingly clear: Elizabeth was not alone. Elizabeth was not the only woman feeling lost and directionless. In fact, women today—despite our education, despite our independence, despite our relationships—have yet to *really* answer the most basic questions about our own identities. Worse still, we seem to have very little idea about how to find them.

The Picket Fence

"I'm Jim's wife, and Janey's mother, a putter on of diapers and snowsuits, a server of meals, a Little League chauffeur. But who am I, as a person myself? —Anonymous Woman*[1]

And yet, if there were ever a generation of women who *should* have a strong sense of their own identity, it is ours. We were the first generation to grow up with empowered mothers; we were the first generation to be taught that we could be whatever we wanted to be. We have had more opportunity, more choices, and more autonomy to make those choices than any women have at any time. If it were simply a matter of making our way in the world, we should have no issues. But we do. And so, in order to understand why we struggle with questions of identity, we first need to understand how our mothers and grandmothers struggled with their own. We need to understand what brought us to this point in the first place.

During the 1950s, Western society was finally experiencing a period of prosperity and stability after nearly two decades of hardship. This generation had been children during the Great Depression and had come of age through the atrocities of World War II, so as adults, they pursued a lifestyle of comfort and security, wanting to provide better for their own children. It was the time of the American Dream, Ward and June Cleaver, the quintessential white picket fence. But this was also a generation schooled in Freudian psychology that promoted the subtle (and at times, not so subtle) idea that identity was primarily discovered and fulfilled through

---

1. Quoted in Betty Friedan, *Life So Far* (New York: Simon & Schuster, 2000), 104.

biology.[2] For a woman, this meant that she should seek her ultimate fulfillment in domesticity, that her identity could be reduced to her "evolutionary" function of being a wife and mother.

But this excessive emphasis on gender couldn't be completely satisfying because it didn't address the deeper questions of existence. It also left women who weren't married, who weren't mothers, or who struggled with domesticity searching for answers to *their* identities—*were they somehow less human because their lives didn't play out in the traditional domestic milieu?* Ultimately the problem wasn't that women devoted themselves to their husbands and children (which itself is *eminently* valuable) but that they were told to look to their husbands and children for their fundamental source of identity.

Hear Me Roar

In response, their daughters (determined, like all daughters, not to turn into their mothers) launched a social movement known as second-wave feminism. They believed that in order to discover full identity, women simply needed to be freed from the bondage of biological roles; personal fulfillment was found in autonomy—whether that meant sexual autonomy in the form of birth control and abortion or economic autonomy through education and a career path. This led them to champion a pro-choice agenda at the same time they were fighting gender discrimination in business and education.

And while there *were* serious societal paradigms that needed to be challenged, second-wave feminism no more successfully

---

2. Sigmund Freud was one of the first to use Darwinian theory to analyze human behavior. He based his work on the premise that "anatomy is destiny" and heavily emphasized the biological differences between men and women, including the idea that women are intrinsically envious of male biology. His theories were widespread in the United States, and by the 1950s, his psychoanalysis was mainstream.

answered the underlying question of personal identity than the previous generation had. Instead of defining themselves by their homes and family, women were now compelled to define themselves by their education, professional accomplishments, and independence from men. While the domesticity of the 1950s may have truncated identity in one respect, subsequent feminist thought simply lopped it off in another.

Neither fully addressed all that it means to be a woman, all that it means to be human.

So here we are—two generations and a world of opportunities later—still wrestling with the same issues. And the reason we are is because we have never really answered the basic questions of identity. Instead, we've tried to answer *how* identity manifests itself without first answering where identity comes from; we've tried to figure out *where* a woman should spend her life without first answering *who* she should be. We've taken shortcuts, and these shortcuts have led us directly to our present confusion and restlessness.

If we are to find any lasting stability in this life, if we are to really answer the question "Who am I and why am I here?" we must move past these easy categories—we must stop talking simply in terms of home vs. career; we must dig deeper than biology or gifting. We must find something more stable, more fixed, more permanent on which to base our sense of self. We must find a North Star. And not simply because our circumstances change, but because we ourselves are more than the roles we play in this present world. We are large, deep, eternal beings, and only something larger and deeper and more eternal will satisfy the questions in our souls.

We need something—Someone—Divine.

The Unknown God

"Without knowledge of self there is no knowledge of God . . .
without knowledge of God there is no knowledge of self."
—John Calvin

Nearly two thousand years ago, on the rugged hillsides of Athens, the apostle Paul encountered a group of people in the middle of their own search for identity. Hoping to connect to the Divine, these seekers devoted themselves to philosophy and religion, worshiping every life force they could identify—and just to hedge the bet, even one they couldn't. Among their columned temples to Athena, Artemis, and Zeus, they had erected an altar to "the unknown god." Recognizing their confusion, Paul stepped forward to remind them of a truth they already knew—a truth that we all in the quiet recesses of our souls already know too.[3]

He told them that "the unknown god" wasn't really unknown but was "the God who made the world and everything in it."[4] He even quoted their own philosophers, reminding them that "in him we live and move and have our being."[5] Simply put, there is one God and He is the Giver of all life. He created the world, and everything in it finds its source, its purpose, and its goal in Him. Including each one of us. Later in a letter to the Corinthian believers, Paul expresses it this way: "There is one God, the Father, from whom are all things and for whom we exist, and one Lord, Jesus Christ, through whom are all things and through whom we exist."[6]

In other words, your identity—everything about you from where you were born to the person you married (or didn't), to

---

3. Romans 1:19–20.
4. Acts 17:24.
5. In Acts 17:28, Paul is most likely quoting the seventh century BC Greek philosopher-poet Epimenides.
6. 1 Corinthians 8:6.

what you love to do, everything that you use to define who you are, everything that you see in the mirror each morning—relates directly and unequivocally to Him.[7] So in order to know yourself, you first have to know Him. In order to know who you are, you must first know who He is. And to do this, you have to go back to the beginning; and not simply back to the beginning of your own individual story, but back to the *very* beginning, the beginning of life itself. Because it is there, in those opening moments of the cosmos, that God first revealed Himself; and it is there that you will first learn what it means to be His daughter.

In the Beginning . . .

But when you do go back, the first thing you'll discover is . . . nothing. Before the ancient hardwood forests, before the vivid northern lights, before the massive heaps of volcanic rock that jut out of the Pacific to form lush tropical islands, Scripture tells us that there was simply nothing. Well, not exactly. Even while our world was empty and dark, even before there was anything on this earth that we would recognize, there was Something. There was Someone. There was God.[8] At that point, He was still mysterious and unknown, but He *was*. And more than simply being present, Scripture tells us that everything that would eventually be already existed in Him—that He Himself was the source of all life and by His very existence, all life continues to this day.[9]

Yet, He never began, was not made by anything else, and cannot be measured.

And *that* is really hard for us number-obsessed humans to understand. We, who mark our days in weeks, months, and years;

---

7. Romans 11:36.
8. Psalm 90:2.
9. Colossians 1:16–17.

who track our bodies in calories, pounds, and BMI; and who can only understand the value of something in dollars, euros, or yen, simply cannot grasp this kind of limitless Being. It's easy to understand why many people turn away from this kind of God and why many of those ancient Athenians turned away from Paul's words too; why they mocked him as they went.

But some did not. Some believed.

And that's what we must do too. In our search for identity, in trying to understand who we are, we must start with Him, yes; but starting with Him requires more than simple logical assent, because quite frankly, sometimes He isn't logical—not to our minds at least.[10] No, starting with Him means accepting Him for who He is, not who we can conceive Him to be. Starting with Him means humbling ourselves to recognize that there is Someone bigger than us who often works in ways we can't explain.

Starting with Him requires faith. Faith that believes He exists and faith that honestly seeks Him, no matter who or what He reveals Himself to be. The epistle to the Hebrews puts it this way: "By faith, we understand that the universe was created by the word of God so that what is seen was not made out of things that are visible . . .Whoever would draw near to God must believe that he exists and that he rewards those who seek him."[11]

Woman Seeking Committed Relationship

Today many of us describe ourselves as seekers much like the ancient Athenians. We question the establishment, critique long-held beliefs, and want proof before we accept the answers. And while doubt can be a healthy thing, we must not trick ourselves into thinking that we are seeking God if we are simply reserving

---

10. Isaiah 55:8–9.
11. Hebrews 11:3, 6.

the right to decide whether or not we approve of the God we eventually discover. This is not faith.

Instead, God asks that you seek Him "with all your heart and with all your soul."[12] That you allow Him to penetrate your defenses, that you allow Him to tear down your preconceived notions, that you allow Him to be simply who He is. And if you do, He promises that you will find Him. *This* is the reward that Hebrews speaks about. When God rewards those who seek Him, it is not with wealth or power or privilege but with the very thing that they were searching for in the first place—Himself.

And the beauty, the unmistakable genius of it all, is that in discovering Him, the source of all existence, you will also discover yourself. In finding Him, you will find the answer to the question "Who am I and why am I here?" Because in the infinite wisdom of God, the two are inextricably linked; and in the infinite kindness of God, this search is as much about His glory as it is your good.

Still, that does not mean it will be easy.

Thankfully, He's the kind of God who welcomes our questions, who can wrestle with us through the confusion and still bless us in the process. He is the kind of God who desires true faith, even at its weakest points, and looks for mustard seeds instead of mountains. He is the kind of God who delights in the plea, "Help my unbelief" and then holds on to us because we can't hold on to Him anymore. He is the kind of God who can handle all our doubt, all our fear, all our questions if we will simply commit to letting Him.

And that is what faith does. Faith does not pretend that it is easy to believe what God reveals about Himself. Faith does not push aside or deny the difficulties. Faith simply commits to taking the questions back to Him and believes that He will have the answers.

---

12. Deuteronomy 4:29; see also Jeremiah 29:13 and Matthew 7:7–8.

The God Who Seeks

One of the most compelling things about this majestic God, this God who existed before the worlds began, is that He understands our weakness. As David sang in the Judean hillsides, "He knows our frame and remembers that we are dust."[13] So much so, that even back in the emptiness of the cosmos, He knew that we would never be able to truly seek Him for ourselves. He knew that in our confusion, we would stumble about in the darkness, unable to find Him and unable to understand ourselves. He knew this, and so in those moments before He laid the foundations of the earth, He planned a way that He would find us.[14]

It's a plan that has unfolded throughout human history, as massive in scale as it is intimate in detail. It's a plan that has often twisted and turned, at times seeming to make little sense. And ultimately it is a plan that took its fullest shape when He Himself came to us in Jesus Christ.

And always, always, it has been a plan to make us like Himself.

You are part of that plan. No matter how far you have wandered or how confused you are or how assured you are that you don't need Him—still, He has planned your life and has been pursuing you since before time began. Before your first breath, before your first cry, before you even knew yourself, He knew you and has been on a mission to make you one with Himself. Because when you finally are, you will finally know Him; and when you know Him, then you will finally be able to *live and move and have your being* as He has always intended. You will finally be free to live beyond the roles and labels and expectations because you will finally be free to live in the fullness of God Himself.

---

13. Psalm 103:14.
14. Ephesians 1:4.

chapter 2

Imago Dei:
Life as It Is Meant to Be

"There are no ordinary people. You have never talked to a mere mortal."—C. S. Lewis

And it was good.

When God was ready to put His Great Plan into action, when He finally stepped out from behind that curtain of darkness, He did so without trumpet or fanfare. There was no press release or opening night gala. In His own subtle elegance, He began with a few simple words: "Let there be light."

And as those words reverberated across the darkness, the world unfurled herself. Light cut through shadow, waters gathered together, and sky and land hedged their boundaries. Next, brushy reeds, forsythia, and lilac carpeted the prairies, woodlands, and craggy mountains. By day, the sky glowed under a majestic sun and at night became a beauty swathed in velvet, decked by diamond studs and pendant moon. Soon fowl and fish, each schooled in their own migratory dances, swarmed in sea and sky. Then, creatures of every shape and dimension emerged from the dust; from the rough-contoured scaly beasts to the petite scampering grey mouse and skittish red squirrel, each came to life at the call of their Master.

And it was good. Very, very good.

There is an unmistakable majesty that throbs and pulses through nature—the kind of wonder that captures you as you gaze into a summer night's sky or stand beside a thundering waterfall. The kind of wonder that makes you both swell with the possibilities this life holds at the same time it makes you shrink back with the knowledge that you are a very, very small part of this massive cosmos.

I remember feeling this one summer when my husband, Nathan, and I drove from Seattle to Los Angeles on Highway 101. We had both been raised in the eastern United States, more at home in the rolling Appalachians than anywhere else, but this summer, we were visiting friends in Seattle and decided to drive down the Pacific coast before flying out of LA. We had been on the road only a few hours when, somewhere in Oregon, we crested a bend and I saw the Pacific Ocean for the first time. I yelled at Nathan to stop the car, quickly jumped out, and ran to a short length of beach. I stood there taking it all in—the waves pounding against the rocky coast, the rough winds whipping my helpless hair, the gulls crying as they somersaulted above the water, and the salt sea biting at my upturned face.

And I felt very small.

Over the next several days, we continued down the coast hedged on our right by a massive, foggy ocean and on our left by towering mountains and ancient forests. And all I could think was how little, how vulnerable, how insignificant I felt. And I realized how easily one person could get lost in all of this, how easily one person could be forgotten. Like David, I couldn't help but think, "What is man that you are mindful of him? And the son of man that you care for him?"[1] And I wondered, *How does one person make any difference in all this?*

---

1. Psalm 8:4.

Specks of Dust

The fear that our lives lack significance, that we are merely specks of dust floating in the massive cosmos, can easily spark the search for identity. When you consider the enormity of the universe, when you realize that Earth itself comprises only an infinitesimal part of it, and when you recognize that you are only one out of the *billions* of people who have lived, it's easy to feel small. Add to this the fact that we must devote vast amounts of time on the basics of daily life (I once calculated that in my lifetime I will prepare nearly 50,000 meals for my family), and it's a wonder we all don't run off to exotic places in search of ourselves!

This fear that we simply trudge through our allotted days without ever making a difference drives some women on a never-ending pursuit of success and perfection. From the fast-paced executive always scrambling for the next deal to the tiger mom bent on shaping her child into a future Supreme Court justice, we are hounded by the thought that our existence will somehow be worthless unless we achieve quantifiable success. For others, this same fear causes them to retreat into their own zone of comfort and hide from the greater world, content to be a big fish in a small pond if it means avoiding the constant reminders of their limitations and irrelevance.

And yet the deeper magic is that no matter how small we may feel—no matter how small we actually may be—we are not insignificant. We are not lost in the grand cosmos. We do matter. But it's not because of anything we've done; it's because of something *God* did back at the beginning. Because back when God created all this beauty, all this life, all this splendor, He capped it off with one final masterpiece—one that He did not leave to words alone. No, for this final masterpiece, He stooped down and left His own fingerprints in the dust.

And that final masterpiece was us.

Crowned with Glory and Honor

"My God, I heard this day / That none doth build a stately
habitation / But he that means to dwell therein. / What house
more stately has there been / Or can be, than is Man?"
—George Herbert, "Man"

Genesis describes the first moments of human existence like this: "Then God said, 'Let us make man in our image, after our likeness . . .' So God created man in his own image, in the image of God he created him, male and female he created them."[2]

Unlike the rest of creation, as majestic and glorious as it is, only men and women are made in the image of God. Only we have the breath, the very spirit of God, flowing in our earthly lungs; only we can be truly called His children.

And this is why your life is significant.

It's not because of what you accomplish or how many people you influence. Your life is significant because when God created you, He "crowned [you] with glory and honor"[3] by making you like Himself. Because as certainly as God formed our first parents, He formed you in your mother's womb,[4] and just as certainly as they bore His image, you bear His image today. As you walk and talk and live and move—and prepare those 50,000 meals—your very existence, your life itself, reflects and represents Him on this earth.

This is where you must find identity—you must find it *imago dei*.

For centuries, philosophers and theologians have used the brief Latin phrase *imago dei* to communicate a hefty truth. Literally translated, *imago dei* simply means "in the image of God." But in reality, *imago dei* means so much more. *Imago dei* means that

---

2. Genesis 1:26–27.
3. Psalm 8:5.
4. Psalm 139:13.

your life has purpose and meaning because God has made you to be like Himself. *Imago dei* means that your life has intrinsic value, not simply because of who you are as an individual, but because of who He is as your God. *Imago dei* means that your life is sacred because He has stamped His identity onto yours.

When Genesis teaches that we are made *imago dei*, it is doing more than simply explaining how we came into existence or offering an argument for why we should respect and care for one another. By revealing that we are made in God's image, it is revealing *how we are to exist*, how we are made to live, and what it means to be human. Being human means sharing God's nature in some way; being human means living as He lives and doing what He does.

In a sense, the image of God is something like DNA. If you remember high school biology (or have watched enough episodes of *CSI*), you'll know that DNA is a chemical substance found in nearly every cell of your body—from the tips of your fingers to the ends of your hair. It is the "secret code" that determines how your cells will develop, what color your eyes will be, whether your hair will be curly or straight, and even more basically, whether you are a lion or a human. And if the need arises, DNA can also identify you, because everything about your physical identity flows directly from it.

Just as your DNA determines what you will look like and how your body will function, being made in God's image determines what you were made to *be* and what you were made to *do*. So when you ask the question, "Who am I and why am I here?" the answer is surprisingly simple. Because you are made in God's image, you exist to reflect and represent Him on this earth. Because you are made in God's image, you are made to proclaim what He is like by doing what He does.

Because you are made in God's image, you are made for glory.

A God-Shaped Heart

"It is the pervading law of all things . . . that form ever follows function."—Louis Sullivan

But as simple as it is to say that you are made to reflect and represent God, unpacking it is not so simple. Because God is a vast, infinitely complex Being, those who are made in His likeness will also be vast and infinitely complex. And yet, Scripture does give us clues about our *imago dei* identity; and it does so in context of the relationships we share with God, with each other, and with creation.[5]

First, finding identity as an image bearer means that you are made to live in dependent communion with God. When God created us in His image, He established a relationship with us that the rest of creation does not share. While creation enjoys a type of fellowship with God—Paul talks in Romans 8 about the earth groaning as it waits for redemption; and Jesus Himself promised that the very stones would cry out in praise to their Creator if the people did not—only human beings live in dependent, personal communion with Him. St. Augustine, a fifth century African bishop, captured this dependency when he wrote, "Thou hast made us for thyself, and our hearts are restless until they rest in Thee." Pastors often communicate the same sentiment when they reference the "God-shaped hole" in the heart of every person that can only be filled by a relationship with Him. That "hole" is the direct result of being made in His image. Apart from Him, you cannot be fully human; apart from Him, you cannot be fully yourself.

Jesus taught something similar during His earthly ministry. Always looking for a way to discredit Jesus' teaching, the Jewish

---

5. I am indebted to Anthony Hoekema who explores this structure more fully in his book *Created in God's Image* (Grand Rapids, MI.: Eerdmans, 1986). He bases the three elements of this paradigm on Genesis 1:26–27.

religious leaders had sent men to ask Him this question: "Is it lawful for us to give tribute to Caesar, or not?"[6] This was a no-win situation; if Jesus answered that the Jews should not pay taxes to Caesar, He risked arrest and punishment as a political zealot. If He answered that they should pay taxes, He risked losing the people's loyalty, and the religious leaders could easily brand Him as unfaithful to Israel and, in a pinch, to Israel's God.

But with divine wisdom, Jesus responded to the question with a question. "Show me a denarius," He said. "Whose likeness and inscription does it have?"

The answer was, of course, "Caesar's."

As the ruler of the known world, Caesar had imprinted his image—his likeness—onto coins. These coins were then distributed throughout his empire and established his authority over each region. Because no one else had the power to make coins, all buying and selling, essentially all the business of life, had to be transacted via his image. It was a subtle, daily reminder to every citizen and every conquered subject that they were dependent on their emperor.

So when the people answered, "Caesar," Jesus replied simply, "Then render to Caesar the things that are Caesar's, and to God the things that are God's."

And with those words, He turned the tables on the religious leaders and propelled the conversation one step further. If God expects us to return to Caesar the things that bear *his* image (in this case, a coin), how much more does He expect us to return to Him the things that bear *His* image: our very selves? By elevating what appeared to be a simple debate about taxes, Jesus taught that part of being made in the image of God means acknowledging His sovereignty in our lives and our dependence on Him.

---

6. Luke 20:19–26.

And this is far more difficult than paying taxes could ever be.

We are people who love our autonomy; our very society is founded on the concept of individuality and freedom. We have so connected the two that we believe that we cannot truly be ourselves if we are tied to someone else. This is why we leave our marriages when we feel stifled and why we want to be alone to find ourselves. Because of this, the dependency that comes from being made in the image of God could sound like a cruel joke or the design of an egomaniacal deity. By making us this way, God ensures that we will never be able to know ourselves apart from Him; and because we can't, He ensures that we cannot live independently of Him.

Our very nature ties us to Him.

But we are not the only ones tied.

He is tied to us. By placing His image in us, God assumes an extra measure of ownership and responsibility for our lives. We are His brand, His trademark. You may remember that the second commandment prohibits making graven images of God. Part of the reason behind this is that God has already graven an image of Himself—in us.

But more than this, by placing His image on us, God has bound Himself to us as a parent. We are His children.[7] And like any good parent, He must protect and nurture His children. The beauty and genius of this is that our good and His glory are inseparable. While our good is found by displaying His glory, His glory is found by bringing about our good.[8]

---

7. In Acts 17:28, Paul reminds the Athenians that "we are His offspring."
8. Romans 9:23.

No Islands

"No man is an island entire of itself.
Every man is a piece of the continent, part of the main."
—*John Donne*

Second, finding identity as image bearers means learning to live in relationship with other human beings. Genesis 2 records that when God made us, He formed the man first and placed him in the midst of His creation. But then He said something puzzling; He said, "It is not good that the man should be alone."[9] Despite the beauty and grandeur of this world, something was missing. So acting on His own command, God formed the woman.

Scripture says, "The Lord God caused a deep sleep to fall upon the man, and while he slept took one of his ribs and closed up its place with flesh. And the rib that the Lord God had taken from the man he made into a woman and brought her to the man."[10]

By doing this, God revealed two fundamental truths about our humanity: (1) both men and women are fully formed, equal image bearers, and (2) we are different from each other and therefore dependent on each other. In other words, while each of us is fully in the image of God, none of us can fully reflect and represent God alone. Instead we reveal the nature of God *together*; and as a result, we also find identity *together*.

We don't always recognize this as we should, in part, because we misunderstand the main reason for the woman's creation. Rather than simply providing the man with a sort of assistant, Scripture records that God formed her in direct response to the fact that the man was *alone*. But this was not loneliness

---

9. Ecclesiastes 4:9–12 also explores the weaknesses of being alone and says that "two are better than one . . . [and] a threefold cord is not easily broken."
10. Genesis 2:21–22.

in the way we commonly understand it; instead his "aloneness" was a deep, persistent sense of isolation and incompleteness that reached every aspect of his identity and directly impeded his ability to live *imago dei*. It was so pervasive that even meaningful work and Eden's abundant plant and animal life could not compensate for the lack of human relationship.

So God created woman. And when the man saw her for the first time, he broke into song. "This *at last* is bone of my bones and flesh of my flesh; she shall be called Woman for she was taken out of Man" (Genesis 2:23).[11] In her, he recognized another human being—not another animal—but a person made in the likeness of God just as he was. And with her, he could live in intimate, daily communion; he could love and be loved.

God's Stewards

Finally, finding identity as image bearers means stewarding creation the way God does. After God made man and woman, He blessed them and entrusted them with caring for His creation. He said, "Be fruitful and multiply, and fill the earth and subdue it; and have dominion over the fish of the sea and over the birds of the heavens and over every living thing that moves on the earth."[12]

Generations later, David echoed this by saying, "You have given him dominion over the works of your hands; you have put all things under his feet."[13] So in a sense, being an image bearer means being God's representative; while He is the ultimate Sovereign, He has delegated authority to us to care and steward what He has created. And we do that the same way He does—by being creative,

11. By making the woman from the man's rib, God shows that she is the same substance and essence as him. In a sense, the rib was a "starter" much the same way that yogurt or sourdough bread begins with a starter.
12. Genesis 1:28.
13. Psalm 8:6.

life-giving people just as He is a creative, life-giving God.

In many ways, this third element of identity flows directly from the first two. If existing in communion with God and others is who you are designed to *be*, then stewarding creation is what you were designed to *do*. And yet, we cannot separate the *being* from the *doing*—a hammer is a hammer both because of how it is shaped and what it accomplishes.

One example of how this being and doing connect is the mystery of conception. Every human being that exists is, in some way, a product of the relationship between a man and a woman. Ideally, this happens in marriage as the love between a husband and wife draws them together in a physical intimacy that mirrors the intimacy of their spirits. Then, when they come together (and as God ordains), a new life begins; *by joining together as image bearers, they form new image bearers just as God did so long ago.*

And this is precisely why it is so breathtaking.

When we see a baby born and when we hear that first cry, we are witnessing not only the miracle of a new life but the miracle of existing as we are intended to exist. In this one moment, the three elements of *imago dei* identity align. As a couple depends (1) on God's grace and (2) they join themselves together in love, they (3) fulfill the call to steward creation by being fruitful and multiplying. The genius is that the very design of our bodies as male and female—who we *are*—is what allows us to *do* what God Himself does. In this one moment, our *being* and our *doing* meet.

But conception is not the only place this happens. Our ability to image God is not dependent on whether we are sexually active or ever conceive a child. Instead it is found in the relationships that we share with Him, with each other, and as stewards over creation. Whether we work as executives, homemakers, educators, or farmers, we all can experience the same breathtaking joy of living as image bearers. Because just as a husband and wife cannot conceive a child without dependence on God and each other, we cannot exercise our creativity—we cannot steward creation—apart from dependence on God and each other. So when you collaborate to make a thing of beauty, when you design a bridge that can support ten thousand tons, when you step back from a project and can say, "That's good," you are doing what God did when He first created. You are living *imago dei*.

The Glory of God

"The glory of God is a human being fully alive; and to be alive consists in beholding God."—Irenaeus

As an image bearer, you are made to reflect and represent God on this earth.[14] And this happens as you live at the convergence of the three aspects of identity. In order to know yourself and exist as you were meant to exist, you must live in dependent communion with Him; you must be in loving relationship with others; and you must exercise creative care over creation. And when any one of these elements is off-kilter, you will experience a loss of identity and feel disoriented simply because you are not existing as you were created to exist.

And yet, when these three elements are working in coordination, you will become fully alive. You will know yourself and God's image will radiate through your life like light radiates through a prism. Each element will act as a plane, and working in coordination with the others, bend His glory through your identity, revealing not only the depth and brilliance of who He is but illuminating your own existence as well. What once seemed so elusive, what you could not see with your naked eye, will suddenly burst forth in a

---

14. As St. Bonaventure wrote, this means you exist, not to somehow "increase His glory, but to show it forth and to communicate it" (St. Bonaventure, In *II Sent.* I, 2, 2, 1).

Technicolor rainbow. And you will finally see.

You will finally see who you are and what you are to do—you will find your identity—because you will finally see the splendor of your great and glorious God.

chapter 3

East of Eden:
When Everything Goes Terribly Wrong

*"It is equally dangerous to know of God without knowing
of one's own rejectedness and to know one's own rejectedness
without knowing God." —Blaise Pascal*

I don't remember when I first realized that this was a broken
world. Or that I was broken person.

When I think about childhood, I remember other things. My
first kitten, the one that looked so much like a powder puff that
even at five I had the prescience to name him Fluff. The apple tree
in my grandma's orchard with its silver-grey bark and low-slung
branches that became a theatre for my girlhood dreams. The freedom of summer nights that lingered and lingered and seemed to
understand that I wouldn't be able to sleep until I'd chased the
first fireflies and felt the grass turn damp under my feet.

Mine was a childhood of lightness and joy, of knowing exactly
where I fit and who I was. I was my father's daughter, a reader
like my mother, and sister to my brothers and long-awaited little
sister. Growing up on ten acres of gorgeous Pennsylvania homestead, I best knew myself when I was wandering the woods in
search of spring's first yellow violets; or walking behind my father

as we planted a year's worth of beans, him digging the furrow and me dropping in a seed every four inches; or sitting on our front porch and watching with wide-eyed wonder as the sun's golden orb dipped behind the distant Appalachian hills painting the sky in warm oranges, purples, and pinks.

I also grew up in other Edens offered up by the likes of Lucy Maud Montgomery and Jane Austen; I imagined myself Nancy Drew, Amy Carmichael, and Lizzie Bennett all rolled into one. You'll understand it when I say that—in many ways—it was easier for me to make sense of identity as a child than it is now as an adult.

And yet, I do remember dark snapshots—the shadows that predicted a world that wasn't as it should be. My dad holding me in his strong arms as he told me that Fluff had been hit by a car. Hiding behind the couch while my parents watched a film about a deformed man who had been displayed as a circus freak in Victorian England and the bedtime fears that accompanied me for weeks after. Or perhaps darkest of all, coming home one day to discover my grandma, so vibrant and full of life, suddenly cold and dead because her heart had stopped.

I don't remember the first time that I realized that this was a broken world, but I haven't been able to escape it since.

Ours is a world of tragic paradoxes. A world where people labor under backbreaking conditions and still are unable to support themselves and provide for their families; a world where vulnerable children are trafficked like animals, bodies and souls sold to the highest bidder; a world where the wealthy waste resources as nations slowly starve to death; a world where men and women routinely destroy themselves through addiction in a desperate attempt to escape the brokenness.

And if we're completely honest, we have to admit that the brokenness isn't simply around us. This brokenness invades our own souls. Instead of God's glory radiating through the prism of our lives, much of the time it is obscured and darkened. Instead of owning our legacy as image bearers, we wander around half-human, or—as a friend of mine recently described it—in a funk. Nothing makes sense, nothing feels at home. Trapped in this awkward fog, we exist in a twilight zone between what we were and what we hope to be.

Yet, the opening chapters of Genesis don't read like this. Instead, they describe a world of promise and expectation, a world where men and women commune with God and each other, fulfilling their destinies as stewards of the earth. All is peace and light. The glory of God quite literally dwells in human flesh. There is no pain; no sorrow. No identity crises.

So what in this world—what in heaven's name—has happened to us?

What in the World Happened

To understand this present brokenness and how it affects the search for identity, we must first understand something else. We must understand what happened to those first image bearers.

After God created the man and woman, He entrusted them with His newly formed paradise. Part of that meant freely exploring and enjoying all that He had made. They were to indulge in the abundance of the garden, to feast on the tree of life and the sweet fruit of every bush, to gorge themselves on wild strawberries and let the juice of ripe mangos trickle down their chins. And then as the sun set, as the grass became damp under their feet, they were invited to walk with Him, to recall the days' joys and say their good-nights while a silvery moon slowly rose over their sleepy garden. In so many ways, they were like children knowing exactly who they were and where they belonged; they were free to be themselves, free to live as God had created them.

But this freedom was dependent on one thing. The man and the woman must not eat from the tree of the knowledge of good and evil. If they did, they would die.

As morbid as it sounds, this wasn't an arbitrary law or the invention of a God desperate to prove His control. Instead, the tree of the knowledge of good and evil represented a source of existence, a source of identity, apart from God. Eating of it would enable the man and woman to discern—to define—reality for themselves.[1]

But because they were created in God's image, they *had* to exist in communion with Him; they *had* to find their understanding of reality from Him alone. If they disobeyed, they would not simply be rejecting Him—they would be rejecting *everything that was true about themselves as well*. By choosing to turn from God to something else for knowledge, they would blind themselves to their own nature. And they would die because they would cut themselves off from the only thing that made them alive in the first place—God Himself.

But part of being image bearers also meant that the man and woman had the ability to act. They were fully dependent on God, but they were not beasts or objects simply to be acted upon. So not only did they need to live in communion with God and others, they also had to choose those relationships for themselves.[2] But they did not. Instead, the image bearers turned traitor and refused to do the very thing they were created to do: they refused to find identity in Him.

---

1. Nancy Guthrie writes, "To eat of it was to assume the right to decide for oneself what is good and what is evil rather than depend on God to define good and evil." Nancy Guthrie, *The Promised One* (Wheaton, IL: Crossway, 2011), 70.
2. One paradox of *imago dei* is that, because we are both body and spirit, we must both obey and *desire* to obey. Philippians 2:13 teaches that God works in us "both to will and to work for" His good pleasure.

The First Identity Crisis

It all started when Satan disguised himself as a serpent and came to the woman in the garden. He began by subtly questioning her understanding of God and of herself. "Did God actually say . . ." he hissed. "Are you sure . . . ?" he asked. He then offered her an alternative identity. In his version, God is not good; He is lying to you. He is threatened by you because you have the power to be like God yourself. You don't have to be an image bearer; you can be the *Image.* Countering God's warning of death, the serpent assured her, "You will not surely die . . . [but] when you eat of it your eyes will be opened, and you will be like God, knowing good and evil."[3]

The tragic irony is that the serpent tempted the woman with something that was already true—made in God's image, she *already was like Him!* She already radiated His majesty and glory; she already existed in perfection. But it was not enough. It was not enough to have His light pulsating through her; she wanted to be the light itself.

So she took the fruit and ate it. Then she offered it to her husband, who was with her, and he ate it too.

And as they indulged, each succulent mouthful became bitterness to their souls. Little did they realize that they were the ones being consumed, they were the ones being devoured. Because as quickly as they had filled their bellies, their spirits were filled with shame; burning, writhing, debilitating shame. Their joy and innocence quickly mutated to a fear and nakedness that reflected the conflict between their nature as image bearers and their choice to live independently of God. It was a kind of cosmic dissonance, a spiritual schizophrenia that, in one disastrous moment, ripped the very fabric of their identity in two.

And we have never been the same since.

---

3. Genesis 3:4–5.

Sons of Adam and Daughters of Eve

"When we run from God, we run away from everything that makes us alive and free. We run away from our own happiness. We leave our place where we belong—close to his heart."—Sally Lloyd-Jones

If you are honest, you know that this brokenness is part of your identity as well. There is a division, a split personality, a longstanding identity crisis rooted in what you were made to be and what you actually are. As children of those first image bearers, we have inherited both their *imago dei* nature and their decision to live apart from God;[4] so that while we all are made in God's likeness, our capacity to live in this reality has been fundamentally corrupted. It's as if a deadly mutation has been introduced into our DNA that now replicates itself in each new strand in each new generation. Or as if someone took a sledgehammer, swung with full force, and brought it crashing down on the prism of your identity. What once perfectly reflected and radiated the glory of God now lies in a pile of broken shards. Light may still bounce off the pieces, but it is not a full or accurate expression of God's nature.

Instead of living in dependent communion with Him, we fight for autonomy and the ability to rule our own lives; instead of loving and serving each other, we manipulate others to serve our own purposes; instead of exercising creative care of the earth, we consume it in our own greed and lust. Instead of unity, there is disunion; instead of harmony, there is brokenness.

But it's not simply that we inherit this warped identity; we also actively embrace it. Every time we look for knowledge about ourselves from something other than God, we perpetuate the cycle of self-destruction. As we continue to live divorced from our true

---

4. Romans 5:12.

identity in God, we lose a sense of who we are; and as we lose a sense of who we are, we continue to live divorced from our true identity. And we end up struggling, grasping, flailing to find something—anything—that will give us a stable sense of self.

Short of the Glory of God

"It is natural for the mind to believe and for the will to love; so that, for want of true objects, they must attach themselves to false."—Blaise Pascal

When the man and woman turned from God, they thought that they would become "wise" enough that they wouldn't need Him, that they would be able to determine reality for themselves. That they could become the center of their own existence. But hidden in Satan's lies was the truth that human beings could never be the center of our own existence—*we are by nature image bearers.* So when we turn from God, when we refuse to base our identity in Him, we are compelled to find it somewhere else because we must reflect *something.* And when we do, we sin.

In Romans 3:23, Paul describes sin[5] as coming "short of the glory of God." In other words, we sin whenever we act in a way that does not reflect His nature, whenever we are not glorious like He is glorious. But rather than a condemnation of our humanity, this is a judgment of our *fallenness*—a judgment of how far we have come from the glory God originally meant for us! We were created for glory, to display the majesty of God's nature in our own; but instead, we now reflect lesser glories.[6]

---

5. Scripture uses many different metaphors to describe the sin that separates us from God including judicial transgression, darkness, and death. I am emphasizing this particular definition in order to understand sin in terms of being image bearers.

6. Romans 1:21–23.

When we turn to other things for knowledge, when we define ourselves by things like our work, our relationships, our giftedness—even our pain—we create an alternative source of identity. And as we image this false god, our very personhood crystallizes around it. Instead of being fully formed, multidimensional people who radiate the complexity of God's nature, we become one-dimensional caricatures, as limited and superficial as the thing that we have devoted ourselves to. And we actually begin to resemble it.

You can see this in

- The mother who invests so much of her identity in her children that when they are grown, she clings to them in unhealthy dependence and continues to live her life through theirs. The parent becomes the child.

- The frugalista who finds her value in her ability to get a bargain but for all her savings doesn't have the generosity to actually use her money for her own or anyone else's benefit. Her soul shrinks to the size of her budget.

- The woman who draws her sense of self from her educational and professional achievements so that despite having a PhD, she doesn't have the wisdom to understand the value of someone who doesn't.

- The missionary who finds her personhood in ministry and her ability to help others but cannot acknowledge her own weakness or accept grace when she needs it.

When we center our identity on these "lesser glories," we become defined by them, and we end up defining reality by them as well. Like our first parents, we use them to establish our own definition of good and evil and judge ourselves and others by it. When we successfully achieve "good," we feel a high, a moment of fullness in our soul. But whenever it is threatened, *we* feel threatened. When it is taken from us, we become depressed and feel like we've lost ourselves because in so many ways, we truly have. Then, in order to maintain our sense of identity, we will succumb to any number of sinful temptations: arrogance, martyrdom, condescension, and parsimony. We become small, angry, insecure people incapable of living in the fullness God intended. Incapable of reflecting His glory.[7]

The *Harper's Bazaar* of Identity

And yet, if there is anything worse than knowing your own brokenness, it is not knowing what you *should* be. We see the effects of sin; we know our lives are less than they should be. We feel the smallness of them. But since we no longer naturally reflect God's image, how do we know what we're supposed to be like? *How do we know what God is like?*

A couple of years ago, I received a complimentary subscription to *Harper's Bazaar*. It's not a magazine I normally read, but I'm a frugal type, so I couldn't pass on free. Plus, I figured I might learn a little something about *haute couture*, how to move my makeup from blah to wow, and discover those seven essential pieces of every woman's wardrobe. (One of which—just for the record—is not a pair of ten-year-old sweatpants.)

When my first issue arrived, I was captivated: the fabrics were luxurious, the models unbelievably svelte, and the designs daring and exotic. I quickly learned how to select the perfect pair of heels and then how to match them to the perfect dress. Add to that

---

7. This is why sin can prompt an identity crisis. When we sin, we lose our core sense of self because we are acting in direct opposition to God's nature, and by extension, our own identity. This is also why James says that "a double-minded man is unstable in all his ways" (James 1:8).

some insider tips about makeup and hair design, and I discovered a whole new level of fashion.

But this knowledge had a dark side. Knowing what was "in" made it obvious that I was "out." My favorite pair of jeans? Soooo a year ago. The handbag I'd picked up on clearance? Definitely last season. I felt paralyzed; as much as I hated learning that my style was subpar, I simply couldn't look away. This repeated itself month after month. Each new issue brought more information and with it a load of critique and judgment. It also stirred in me a desire for things that I didn't have. Before *Harper's Bazaar*, fashion success meant being fully dressed before the children barged into my bedroom. After the magazine entered my world, I felt intimidated, ugly, and all too "mommyish." But even as I realized I couldn't measure up to those images of beauty and glamour, I felt compelled to try.

My complicated relationship with *Bazaar* was based on this universal truth: *We can't really know how short we come until we know the standard.* So too, we can't know what we are created to be, we can't know what it means to live as image bearers, apart from clear, direct revelation from God. We can't know ourselves apart from His perfect Law as it is revealed in Scripture.

The "L" Word

Hearing about God's Law might conjure for you an image of an unapproachable God, raining down thunder and lightning from atop a storm-shrouded mountain. Maybe you think of the 613 commands that were the foundation of Jewish culture, everything from not eating shellfish to not wearing garments made from two different fabrics. Or maybe you push back against the idea of Law because you come from a background that saw the Scripture as nothing more than a set of rules to obey—a set of rules that seemed constantly out of your reach.

The confusion surrounding the Law is understandable because the Scripture itself speaks about it in many different ways; depending on the context, the Law can refer to the entirety of God's revelation about Himself, the Ten Commandments, or simply the Jewish civil law. When I refer to God's Law here, I'm talking about the fact that God has established boundaries for us that are consistent with our nature as image bearers. In this sense, the first time God gave the "law" wasn't on Mt. Sinai but in Eden. And since then, "at many times and in many ways,"[8] God has continued to reveal Himself through these boundaries. And because these boundaries reveal His nature, they also reveal our own.[9]

Think about what the Law accomplished for the nation of Israel. When God first rescued the Israelites from slavery in Egypt, He began by introducing Himself as "I Am," the one true, sustaining source of existence. And then to teach them more about who He was—to teach them who they were as His image bearers—He gave them boundaries just as He has given them to their first parents so many years before. Instead of a barrier to keep us from being ourselves, God's Law is intended to guide us back to our true ourselves. Sally Lloyd-Jones puts it in words simple enough for a child to understand: "God's rules are his gift to us. To help us be who we really are."[10]

But God's Law does something else for us. God's standards, His expectations show us both what we should be and how far we

---

8. Hebrews 1:1.

9. Theologians refer to this understanding of law as the "moral law" to distinguish it from the Jewish civil and ceremonial law. In Romans 2:15, Paul teaches that this same law has been "written on [the] hearts" of all men regardless of culture or religion. And in *The Abolition of Man*, C. S. Lewis charts key elements of the moral law that can be found cross-culturally.

10. Sally Lloyd-Jones, *Thoughts to Make Your Heart Sing* (Grand Rapids, MI: ZonderKidz, 2012), 54.

come short. In Romans 7, Paul writes that "if it had not been for the law, [he] would not have known sin." And Eugene Peterson paraphrases this same text by writing:

> Without its clear guidelines for right and wrong, moral behavior would be mostly guesswork. Apart from the succinct, surgical command, "You shall not covet," I could have dressed covetousness up to look like virtue and ruined my life with it.[11]

Apart from God's Law, we would ruin ourselves because we would keep living in direct opposition to what we were made to be.

To Redeem Those under the Law

And yet, frustratingly, just like when I flipped through those pages of *Bazaar*, I know I am utterly incapable of doing what the Law asks of me. I know I must embrace God's nature; I feel it in my very being. His Spirit calls out to my spirit. His nature calls out to mine. At the same time, I cannot. Even as my body and soul long for God, I am completely, utterly incapable of doing the very thing that I long to do. Paul expresses this frustration in Romans 7:19 when he writes, "I do not do the good I want, but the evil I do not want is what I keep on doing." Like Paul, *I am completely, utterly incapable of being the very thing I was made to be!*

So because I can't, Christ becomes it for me.

The God who made us, the God who fashioned us out of the dust to display His glory, will not leave His image bearer helpless and broken. When the time was right, He came as a child to rescue His children. Because we had left Him, He came to us. Because we would not humble ourselves, He humbled Himself.

---

11. Romans 7:7–9, *The Message*, copyright © by Eugene H. Peterson 1993, 1994, 1995. Used by permission of NavPress Publishing Group.

Because we would not obey, He obeyed perfectly. And because we live lives of death, He lived and died to free us from them.

Once again, He can proclaim that there is no life apart from Him. There is no existence, no purpose, no reality apart from Him. Because in this moment—when the Image bears the sins of the image bearer—He once again declares that "from Him and through Him and to Him" are all things. He once again declares that He is all in all.

And in this moment, He turns identity upside down.

chapter 4

Made Like Him:
Finding Your Life by Losing Yourself in Him

"His becoming what we are enables us to become what He is."—Irenaeus

During our first eleven years of marriage, Nathan and I moved eight times. And each time, we encountered the same problem—too many books.

Like any addiction, it started out innocently; pick up one at the Goodwill, find another on sale at Amazon, exchange them for birthdays and Christmases—but before we knew it, we found ourselves schlepping boxes and boxes of books cross-country and leaving kitchen chairs behind because there simply wasn't enough room for everything.

Packed in those boxes were a sizeable number of children's books, including several by Eric Carle. Carle is best known for his gentle stories inspired by nature and the colorful collages that accompany them. His artwork has won him international recognition as an illustrator and made his books children's classics. Not everyone's a fan for the same reasons, though. Our six-year-old son, the realist of the family, once told me, "Mommy, I love Eric Carle's books. He is such a good writer . . . his pictures aren't that good, but his words are just perfect."

Carle's most famous book is undoubtedly *The Very Hungry Caterpillar*; in it, a tiny and (quite appropriately) hungry caterpillar eats his way through the days of the week. He munches and chews and gnaws until he eventually feels full and finally wraps himself in a drab cocoon. The story climaxes when the now not-so-hungry--but-rather-fat protagonist suddenly bursts forth from his cocoon as a dazzling butterfly!

Carle is not the first artist to explore the mystery of metamorphosis, the process in which a living creature undergoes dramatic change within its life cycle. Throughout history, from the Romans to the Aztecs, the caterpillar-turned-butterfly has been a metaphor for writers, painters, and mystics who saw the process as essential to the human experience. It was often linked to death and the release of the soul from the body; the Greeks even used the same word, *psyche,* for both butterfly and soul.

Not surprisingly the concept of metamorphosis—or identity shift—is also a central theme of Scripture, but with a difference. In a distinctively Christian paradigm, change doesn't happen as we eat our way through our problems to emerge as a glorious butterfly. And it doesn't simply happen when we die and are released from the cares of life. *Change happens when the God of the universe comes down into the lives of His children, when God meets us where we are and transforms us.* And when He does, shepherds become kings, fishermen preachers, and liars and deceivers? Children of God.

Identity Shift

"Made like Him, like Him we rise, Alleluia!"—Charles Wesley

Yet, the greatest identity shift Scripture records is not one you'd anticipate. In fact, it was so counterintuitive that when it happened, it altered the very fabric of the universe. The greatest identity shift that has ever happened was when God Himself became human and lived and died for us so we once more might live in Him.

The apostle John opens his gospel with these words:

> In the beginning was the Word, and the Word was with God and the Word was God . . . and the Word became flesh and dwelt among us, and we have seen his glory, glory as of the only Son from the Father, full of grace and truth.[1]

The "Word" John is referring to is Jesus of Nazareth. And while most people will quickly acknowledge that Jesus was a gifted teacher and a model of humanity, He is so much more. He is "the radiance of the glory of God and the exact imprint of his nature."[2] He is both the Image and the perfect Image Bearer, the Creator who deigns to live in His own creation. Despite being God, Jesus humbled Himself, took on human flesh, and came to live and die so that through His very life, death, and resurrection—through His metamorphosis—we ourselves might be changed.[3]

As image bearers, our identity is so fundamentally flawed that no amount of metaphysical therapy or healthy living can heal us.[4] Like the caterpillar, our old selves must die.[5] And this begins when we hide ourselves, when we cocoon ourselves in Him. When we humbly admit our brokenness. When we repent, not of our humanity, but of *trying to root our humanity in anything but God Himself.* When we repent of the arrogance that would elevate any created thing above the Creator. When we repent of pursuing things that are not worthy, not large enough, not glorious enough to display His greatness.

---

1. John 1:1, 14.
2. Hebrews 1:3.
3. Philippians 2:6–7.
4. Jeremiah 17:9 describes the human heart as "deceitful" and "desperately sick."
5. Romans 6:6–7.

When we repent of not honoring Him as God.

The paradox of personal identity is that once we accept that we are not what we should be, we are finally in a place to be made what we could be. Once we acknowledge that we are dead apart from God, we are finally able to live in Him. Once we admit the inadequacy of our lives, we are finally able to discover the sufficiency of His.

And this is what Christ offers us. He offers us His identity; He offers us Himself. When we are joined to Him, when our lives are "hidden with Christ in God,"[6] we can finally die to our old selves because as His image bearers, *we become whatever He is.* When He died carrying the weight of sin in His body, we died with Him. When He was buried, we were buried with Him. And when three days later, God raised Him up in resplendent glory, we were raised up in the same glory, to the same newness of life.[7] And like the caterpillar turned butterfly, we are transformed.

This is heavy stuff and on the surface may seem entirely impractical. After all, what significance does the fact that Jesus died and rose again have on your search for identity? How can a man who lived two thousand years ago make any difference in your daily life? The truth is that the heaviest things are often the most practical things: Their weight is the gravity that holds everything else in place.

Because while the sun might seem distant, there is, in fact, nothing more day to day, nothing more necessarily useful than that giant orb of burning gas that is 93 million miles away. And just as the pull of the sun keeps all the planets of the solar system from flinging off into cosmic oblivion, the truth that God came in the form of Jesus keeps everything about your identity in place

---

6. Colossians 3:3.
7. Romans 6:5–11.

as well. And just as the sun provides warmth and stability as our days and years play out under its risings and settings, the fact that Jesus is the perfect Image Bearer provides the stability that we need to live *imago dei*. That the Creator came to His creation, that the Everlasting One lived and died for you, that Jesus offers you a new identity through His . . . is the most practical, the most real thing that you will ever encounter.

Because in those hidden moments of the grave, God transforms us and brings us to life again. The God who first said, "Let there be light," again calls for the light of Christ to shine into our lives.[8] The God who, at the dawn of creation, stooped down into the mud to shape us in His image, again stoops into the mire of our lives to shape us in His image through Christ.[9] Through Him, then, we are made alive. Through the breath of His Spirit, we again breathe. And through His resurrection, we are reborn!

Born to Live

"I am the resurrection and the life. Whoever believes in me, though he die, yet shall he live, and everyone who lives and believes in me shall never die."—Jesus Christ

Like many folks who grew up in the church, I became aware of these metaphysical realities very young. Words like "sin" and "God" were as natural a part of my vocabulary as "please" and "thank you." In fact, they were so much a part of my consciousness that I remember a teacher chiding me as a six-year-old when she mistook my awareness for religiosity. She had asked our class to think about what different colors represented to us. What did we think about when we saw the color blue or orange or yellow? I

---

8. 2 Corinthians 4:6.
9. 2 Corinthians 5:17.

eagerly raised my hand and said, "Every time I see the color red, I think about Jesus dying on the cross."

"No, you don't," she replied curtly. And then as if suddenly aware of her judgmentalism, she added, "Not every time."

I knew better than to argue with her; but as she moved on to a student who would offer a less pious answer, all I could think was, *Yes! Yes, I do!*

My understanding had been shaped, in large part, by early and repeated exposure to the Wordless Book, a teaching aid that used colors to represent spiritual truths. Instead of containing words, each page has a different color to prompt you to think of a corresponding spiritual reality. The page representing Christ's death on the cross? A brilliant, breathtaking red.

The reason I had been exposed to these particular ideas so young was because our church tradition placed a strong emphasis on the moment of conversion, the moment when a person recognizes his or her brokenness and turns to Christ. As a result, we devoted significant time to helping each of us—young and old alike—achieve this moment. Unfortunately, this emphasis sometimes led to neglecting a fuller understanding of what it meant to find identity in Christ. It wasn't uncommon for people to think that this happened only at one moment in time. Their relationship with Him could be pinpointed on a calendar or marked by a date written in the front of their Bibles when they had been "born again."

What many didn't understand was that being born is only the start of living.

When Jesus said that "you must be born again,"[10] He was speaking about when and how spiritual life *begins*, not where it ends. Because while it is true that we cannot live unless we are born, it is also true that our lives cannot be reduced to the moment we enter

10. John 3:7.

this world and breathe our first breath. Finding identity in Christ cannot be confined to one moment, because union with Christ is not simply an event; it is a state of being, a way of existing. When we are united with Christ, He becomes the source of our life.[11] He is our lifeblood, pulsing through our veins; He is our breath and the air we breathe.

We are not only reborn in Him. We *live* in Him!

With St. Patrick, the fourth-century pastor, missionary, and saint, we affirm, we desperately proclaim, that in order to know ourselves—in order to be what we were created to be—Christ must be the center of our being. Christ must be the center of our identity.

> Christ with me, Christ before me, Christ behind me,
> Christ in me, Christ beneath me, Christ above me,
> Christ on my right, Christ on my left,
> Christ when I lie down, Christ when I sit down,
> Christ in the heart of every man who thinks of me,
> Christ in the mouth of every man who speaks of me,
> Christ in the eye that sees me,
> Christ in the ear that hears me.
>
> I arise today through a mighty strength,
> The invocation of the Trinity,
> Through a belief in the Threeness,
> Through a confession of the Oneness
> Of the Creator of creation."[12]

And suddenly Paul's words in Acts 17:28 to the seekers on that Athenian hillside make sense too. Suddenly we understand what union with Christ means for our identity: *"In Him we live and move and have our being."*

---

11. John 15:5.
12. The Lorica of St. Patrick.

Becoming Who We Are

And the promise of the gospel is that as we are united with Christ, as we abide in Him, He will make us like Himself. He will progressively transform every part of us until we become what we were created to be—people who display and radiate the glory of God.[13]

Yet, this is a process we navigate by faith.

Most of us believe, like our first parents, that we can only find our true selves and live full, complete, happy lives if we are free of restraints. You are told to follow your heart, to be true to yourself, to throw off anything that would hold you back—whether that is your own insecurities, marriage vows, or other people. Elizabeth Gilbert thought that she would find herself by leaving her husband and traveling the world. Second-wave feminists thought that women could find themselves in autonomy by breaking the shackles of social constructs and pursuing financial and bodily independence. And some warn us that commitment to Jesus can result only in repression, denial, and a loss of personal identity. The message is simple: you will only truly be yourself if you pursue what *you* want and what *you* love.

But faith teaches us that we will never be more truly ourselves than as we are conformed to God's nature through Christ. Faith teaches us to forgo a superficial authenticity in order to find a deeper, more authentic sense of self. Faith teaches us that we are made to reflect the heart of God.

This is the call of Christ. This is the call of the gospel. Christ promises that "if anyone would come after me, let him deny himself and take up his cross and follow me. For whoever would save his life will lose it, but whoever loses his life for my sake will find it."[14]

And yet, Christ is not calling us to asceticism or legalistic denial

13. Romans 8:29.
14. Matthew 16:24–25.

of our personhood in exchange for some ethereal reward. He is not calling us to lives of duty and obligation merely so one day we will land in heaven. Instead, Christ is calling us to the abundant life[15] that only He can offer; He is calling us to find our deeper selves—the part of ourselves that was created to be like God. He is calling us to a violent authenticity that willingly crucifies our corrupt selves in order that we might finally know our true purpose.[16] In order that we might finally know Him.

He is calling you to faith. Faith to believe that He made you to be so much more than your momentary desires. Faith to believe that He made you to be more than your brokenness, more than your sin. Faith to believe that authenticity means faithfulness to the deepest part of His nature. Faith to believe that you were made for glory.

Faith to believe that this only happens through Christ.

This then is also the promise of the gospel: *You will find yourself by losing yourself in Him.* When you commit yourself to Christ, He will make you the purest, most authentic version of yourself. As He removes your sin, He will strip away the things that have kept you from reflecting His glory and having your existence illuminated by His. And as He does so, you will regain a complete sense of self. You will finally become someone who can embrace your unique identity in order to display the richness of His glory—in order to love Him and serve others with humility and grace.

Instead of indulging in the fruit of the tree of the knowledge of good and evil, we must feast on Him. We must sustain ourselves on the ripe, luscious fruit of His nature—His love and joy and peace and patience and kindness and goodness and faithfulness and gentleness and self-control.[17] And as we do, as we consume

---

15. John 10:10.
16. Ephesians 4:22–24.
17. Galatians 5:22–23.

His identity—as He literally dwells in us—His Spirit will produce this same bountiful harvest in our lives as well.

And then we will know what it means to be alive. Then we will know what it means to be ourselves.

The Rest of the Story

The rest of this book is dedicated to unpacking this truth. The next chapters attempt to unite metaphysical realities with tangible ones, to connect attributes of God's identity to your own. We will explore how God's love is the defining mark of His existence and how as His child, love must define yours as well. We will wrestle with accepting the things about personal identity that are beyond our control but that were always well within His. We will explore what it means to be a complete person living holistically precisely because He does.

The paradigm is simple: God intends to reflect His identity through your identity. What He is, you will become. He is holy; you must be holy.[18] He loves; so you must love.[19] He forgives; so you must forgive.[20] And because He is glorious, you must be glorified as well.

And yet, these are no longer legalistic demands placed upon us, demands that constantly mock our failure and inadequacy. They are not demands; they are His *promises*—promises that He is fulfilling through Jesus Christ. His promise that as we center our identity on Him, as we live lives dependent on His nature, He will live in us. His promise that He will be a well of life, bubbling up inside of us, overflowing to life for all around us. His promise that He will give us the strength to both will and do His good pleasure.

---

18. 1 Peter 1:15.
19. 1 John 4:19.
20. Ephesians 4:32.

His promise that through Him we will finally be the image bearers we were meant to be.[21]

That through Him, we will finally, fully be human.

21. Colossians 3:10.

| *...and Through Him...*

Too often as women, we have restricted
ourselves to the "pink" parts of the Bible.

When we identify first and foremost as women,
we can begin to believe that knowledge
of ourselves will come primarily through
passages that speak to women's issues or
include heroines like Ruth or Esther.

But when we do this, when we craft our
learning and discipleship programs around
being "women," we make womanhood the
central focus of our pursuit of knowledge
instead of Christ.

chapter 5

Looking for Love:
How Your Heart Makes You Who You Are

"To say that I am made in the image of God is to say that love is the reason for my existence, for God is love. Love is my true identity. Selflessness is my true self. Love is my true character. Love is my name."—*Thomas Merton*

Nathan, my husband, is a Virginia boy, born and bred. He grew up in a one-stoplight town in the western part of the state, and while he looks like any other human being, I know for a fact that the Appalachians run down his spine and mountain streams course through his veins. His soul is the birthright of gentlemen farmers, mountain men, and daring patriots.

But when we met in college, we were both ready for more—ready to experience the world, to travel, to live in bigger places. What neither of us knew is that Virginia boys are born with a homing device planted deeply inside them so that no matter where we went, he could never really settle. No other place was quite like home. The years we spent in the flat, patient landscape of northern Indiana nearly did him in, so as soon as possible, he led us back to those green, rolling hills. Today we're raising our children here, and I watch as "Virginia" seeps into their little bodies and returns from them in the form of distinct regional "Yes, ma'ams" and hands and knees stained with rusty earth.

One of the first things that you learn about this commonwealth (because yes, Virginia is a commonwealth) is that "Virginia is for Lovers." Launched originally as a tourism slogan, this statement captures all that I've discovered to be true about Nathan—the passion, the draw, the *desire* of this place. And yet, this passion is not unique to Virginians. Truth be told, we are all lovers. But not in a romantic, colloquial sense. When I say that we are all lovers, I'm describing something deeper, something more fundamental about our identity as human beings. When I say that we are lovers, I mean that being image bearers means that we are made to love—that love is the fundamental way we navigate the world.

People as Lovers

"The things that we love tell us what we are."
—St. Thomas Aquinas

Since the seventeenth century, Western society has operated on a model of personal identity that strongly emphasizes the mind. Most of us recognize René Descartes's axiom "I think, therefore I am," which embodies this approach. Because of this, we tend to understand ourselves in terms of what is happening inside our head. We consult therapists to help us unpack memories; we read books about behavior modification and believe in the power of positive thinking. Within the church, this mindset has also shaped how we engage the process of personal transformation; that is, the process of being made more like God and imaging Him. Because we understand people primarily as "thinkers," we expect change to happen through their minds; this means that for many of us, spiritual growth has become synonymous with books, workshops, blogs, and lectures.[1]

---

1. There is a legitimate call to "renew our minds," which I will address in chapter 7.

James K. A. Smith challenges this idea in his book *Desiring the Kingdom*, and says that when we base our identity simply on what is happening inside our heads, we run the risk of adopting a bobblehead persona. Instead of being fully formed people who reflect God's relational nature, we end up becoming walking dictionaries or catechisms, overflowing with facts and propositions wherever we go. Truthfully, most of us recognize that this "heady" approach has its limitations—especially if you have ever tried to conquer a stubborn sin by doing yet another Bible study or memorizing enough verses. It doesn't take long to recognize that while knowledge of God is a necessary first step, knowledge alone cannot transform you. Because even though you may *know* what you should do, it is rarely what you *want* to do.

Instead Smith argues that "to be human is to love, and it is what we love that defines who we are. Our (ultimate) love is constitutive of our identity."[2] In other words, because we are fundamentally lovers, what we *love* makes us who we are and shapes what we do. This isn't surprising when we remember that God is the ultimate source of our identity. In his first epistle, John makes this simple but startling statement: "God is love" (1 John 4:8). In fact, love is so essential to God's nature that it drove Him to sacrifice Himself so we could be restored to relationship with Him.[3] It was God's love—His very essence—that compelled Him to rescue us.[4]

And because He is love, we are made to love as well.[5]

Remember that Genesis 1 defines being image bearers in context of *relationships*; being human means living in dependent

---

2. James K. A. Smith, *Desiring the Kingdom* (Grand Rapids, MI: Baker Academic, 2009), 51.
3. John continues the thought in v. 9 by saying that "the love of God was made manifest among us, [in] that God sent his only Son into the world, so that we might live through him."
4. John 3:16.
5. 1 John 4:19.

communion with God, in relationship with others, and in stewardship of creation. Because God is relational, we are relational as well. So it's also not surprising that Scripture uses the word "heart" to describe the "inner core of the person,"[6] the *real* you. It's also why Solomon warns to "keep your *heart* with all vigilance, for from it flow the springs of life."[7] And why nearly a thousand years later, Jesus taught the same truth when He said that "the good person out of the good treasure of his *heart* produces good, and the evil person out of his evil treasure produces evil."[8] Because you are fundamentally a lover, what you love will determine who you are and what you do.

So what if the real you isn't found inside your head but about eighteen inches lower? What if the real you is found in what you love? If it is, then the first step to finding identity as an image bearer is figuring out what you love now and learning to love the way God does.

Figuring Out What You Love

Nathan and I married right out of college, and because of this, our first years together were a funny combination of sorting through the mysteries of marriage at the same time we were trying to figure out how the adult world worked. As a result, we developed a running list we simply called "Anderson Rules of Life." These rules ranged from Rule #4: Upturned buckets left outside will fill with rainwater and breed mosquitoes; to Rule #17: If you want to talk to someone in another room, don't shout; walk to the other room. And at the top of our list was Rule #1: People do what they want.

---

6. Anthony A. Hoekema, *Created in God's Image* (Grand Rapids, MI: Eerdmans, 1986), 172.
7. Proverbs 4:23.
8. Luke 6:45.

One of the hardest things about transitioning to adulthood was reconciling why people do what they do. I remember being surprised and disappointed when friends made poor decisions—when they suddenly left their marriages or abused their positions of authority—and I found myself needing to know, "Why—why did you do this?!"

I suppose I was grappling with the loss of my own innocence, but the only answer I could find was that people do what they want; they pursue what they love. The corollary to Anderson Rule of Life #1 is that you can discover what a person loves—where she finds identity—by observing the choices she makes. More significantly, you can discover what you love—where you find identity—by observing the choices you make. Initially this may seem simplistic, and you may object that there are always extenuating circumstances, that no one's choices are made in a vacuum. What about the woman who stays in a dysfunctional relationship? Or the man who hates his job but never quits? Do they *love* these situations?

Because people are exceptionally complicated, the answers to what they love will never be simple. Like untangling a skein of yarn, you must keep pulling, keep tugging on a particular thread until you find the source of the knot. When a woman stays in a dysfunctional relationship, she does not stay because she loves the dysfunction (in fact, she may desperately hate it and hate herself for enduring it), but she stays because she values, for whatever complicated reasons, something the relationship offers her more than she hates the brokenness of it. She may convince herself that staying is easier than risking the unknown; or she believes that the worst father is better than no father for her children; or she thinks that no one else will love her; or a whole host of other things that somehow, in her mind, compensate for the brokenness. The same is true for someone in a job he hates. He may drag himself to work every day and promise himself that today's the day that he gives his two weeks' notice, but he never does because the job provides something else he wants. Whether it is money or security or simply the chance to work in a certain field, his job provides something that he doesn't want to lose.

So when you are sorting through your own life, you must tug on the string. To discover what you love, what drives you and what ultimately gives you your sense of identity, you need to probe past superficial answers. You must ask yourself both what do I do and *why* do I do it? You must ask yourself,

- What do I spend my time doing?
- What do I think about most?
- What do I talk about?
- What do I fight to protect?
- What can make me angry?
- What will I sin to achieve?

And when you pull on that string, when it finally starts to unravel, you will most likely discover that you don't love what or how God loves. You will most likely discover that you don't reflect His character the way you should. You will most likely discover that you don't image Him. And yet, in order to truly be yourself, you must. You must love what and how He loves.

Loving Like God Loves

The most fundamental way that we fail to reflect God's love is either (1) we love the wrong things or (2) we love the right things in a wrong way. Instead of focusing our affections outward toward God and others, we focus them inward, loving ourselves supremely and pursuing the things that we believe will make us happy. Sometimes we can even mask this narcissism with good things—the love of family, a commitment to good works, or even a staunch defense of the faith can all be rooted in self-love if we use them to fulfill desires that only God can.

So in order to restore us, in order to make us the fully faceted people we were meant to be, Christ must change what and how we love.[9] He must reshape and reorder our loves to their proper places. And to do that, He must first hold the central place in our affection.

Jesus taught that the greatest commandment is to love God supremely and that the second greatest is to love our neighbor as ourselves.[10] Because God is supreme, we must desire Him and His approval above anything else; we must position Him as the source of our affections and acceptance; and when we do, as His image bearers, we will naturally reflect His perfect love. This is why the Scripture speaks of our new identity in terms of having a "new heart." When Christ has first place, when we are consumed with His love, we will naturally love like He does.

And yet, unlike some believe, loving God supremely does not mean that we don't love other things; instead it means that we love other things the way that God intends for them to be loved. This is why the second commandment follows on the heels of the first. You can only love your neighbor properly—you can only love him or her as God does—if you find your source and definition of love from God Himself. In this sense, loving your neighbor actually flows out of loving God and cannot happen in the fullness that God intends apart from Him.

One of the greatest sources of joy in my life is parenting our three young children. It is also one the greatest sources of chaos in my life as well. Yet, I find I can handle the messes, the sleepless nights, and

---

9. 1 John 2:15.
10. Matthew 22:36–40.

even the 50,000 meals I'll prepare for them, but what I can't handle is the bickering. The constant picking. The small arguments over who had what first and who took apart whose Legos and why must brothers be so annoying. (I am seriously thinking about forgoing traditional baby gifts from now on. Instead I'm going to start giving something more eminently suited to parenting—a black-and-white striped jersey and a whistle.) In the midst of the chaos, I often find myself yelling at the top of my lungs, "Will you all just stop it?!?! Why can't you just be KIND to each other?"

During one such meltdown, I had an epiphany. Here I was demanding that my children love like God loves without directing them to Him as the source of that love. And yet, the only way my children—those little image bearers themselves—will ever be able to love one another properly is as they encounter and bask in God's love for them first. In a twisted irony, my call for them to love had morphed into legalism because I had presented it apart from the source of love.

Most of the time we associate legalism with strict adherence to a specific set of rules, but legalism is not simply choosing the letter of the law over the spirit. Legalism is any attempt to model God's attributes apart from a relationship with Him. *Legalism is trying to be an image bearer without relying on the Image.*

When we attempt to "love" apart from God, our love will only be as lasting as the current situation or our own ability to sustain it. This is why forced tolerance, political correctness, and the "just be kind" approach often feel so weak and at times, so artificial. These approaches *are* artificial because they are not rooted in *imago dei* relationship. It's like we're playing dress-up in our mother's heels and pearls—clumping down the hallway, mimicking her behavior but never truly embodying it.

But when we are transformed by intimate daily dependence on the Creator's love, when He becomes the *source*, not simply the model, of the love we extend to each other, we will have vast reservoirs of love welling up inside us, overflowing for all. So the way that we come into full personhood, the way that we love as we were intended to love, is not simply to mimic God's love, but to allow it to transform us from the inside out. And then, only then, will people know we are His disciples. They will know we belong to Him because our identity will be consumed by His; they will know we belong to Him because we will love like He loves.[11]

What We Mean When We Talk about Love

"What people mean when they say that God is love is often something quite different: they really mean 'Love is God.'"—C. S. Lewis

But this begs the question, how does God love? How do we know what God's love looks like? In today's society, love means anything from romance to sentimentalism to physical desire. About the only thing we can agree on is that love is affection for something or someone. We might even agree that true love—love that mirrors God's love—is fundamentally directed outward. It is the desire for the well-being of another person. Even true, romantic love must be rooted in seeking the good of the other person.

During His earthly ministry, Jesus described love this way: "Whatever you wish that others would do to you, do also to them."[12] Later He taught in eerily prophetic tones that love would even motivate someone to die for his friends.[13] And then in 1 Corinthians 13, Paul gives us this classic text on how love behaves.

Love is patient and kind;

---

11. John 13:35.
12. Matthew 7:12.
13. John 15:13.

love does not envy or boast;
it is not arrogant or rude.
It does not insist on its own way;
it is not irritable or resentful;
it does not rejoice at wrongdoing,
but rejoices with the truth.
Love bears all things,
believes all things,
hopes all things,
endures all things.
Love never ends.

But there's another aspect of love that we often overlook. One that at first seems counterintuitive and to some, the very opposite of love. But it is also an aspect of love that is essential to our ability to image God as we should. And it is this: true love—love that mirrors God's love—is love that obeys.

If You Love Me

"Therefore be imitators of God as beloved children. And walk in love, as Christ loved us."—Ephesians 5:1–2

When you understand that God's commands are an expression of His nature,[14] you can begin to understand why Jesus said that all the commandments are summed up by loving God with your heart and soul and strength and loving your neighbor as yourself. If God is love, His commands reflect this and by obeying them,

---

14. We must be certain to differentiate between God's Law and the additional laws that people often place upon one another. While Jesus perfectly kept God's Law, He had no qualms about confronting those who placed "heavy burdens" on other people (Matthew 23:4). He also taught that the goal of God's Law is not to enslave people but to free them (Mark 2:27).

we align ourselves both to Him and to one another. This is also why John says that when we have been changed by God's love, His commands are not burdensome.[15] *They are not burdensome because they become the very things that we want for ourselves.* When we are transformed by Christ, when our nature is increasingly like His, we will love what He loves. And as a result, we will do what He does. We will obey the same Law that is an expression of His very nature.

One reason that we struggle with this concept is because we tend to create a false dichotomy between God's Law and His Love. We may see the God of the Old Testament as a tyrannical despot who is only softened by the kind Jesus of the New. In this paradigm, it's easy to view love as a sort of trump suit. When truth and love seemingly conflict, love wins. When righteousness and love seemingly conflict, love wins. Lay down an ace of God's holiness, and I'll trump it with a two of His love.

But this misunderstands the nature of love and of God Himself. Because God is love, He is not self-serving.[16] His Law was never intended for His own benefit, but for *ours*. It is His *love* that compels Him to pursue what is best for His children; and what is best for us is that we would exist in intimate, dependent relationship with Him and one another—that we would become what we were created to be. And we do that by living the way He does; by conforming to His character as it is revealed through His Law and embodied in Christ.

In this sense, love does not negate the Law; love fulfills it.[17]

The beauty is that loving relationship becomes both the means and the end of personal identity. It is both how we exist and the goal for which we exist. We act out of love for God; and our obedience actually causes us to love more because it brings us into

---

15. 1 John 5:3.
16. 1 Corinthians 13:5.
17. Matthew 5:17.

harmony with His nature and our own.

And we see this most clearly in the person and work of Jesus Christ. In Him, grace and truth meet; in Him, love and justice join in perfect union. In Him, we discover that loving like God does not mean finding a balance between two extremes but in discovering the depth of what love truly is. His love is not a muted, muddied love, a milky attempt to negate holiness with kindness, but an infinitely complex, nuanced expression of what it means to love like God. Of what it means to be fully human. The Jesus who chastised the religious leaders for their hard hearts, for their shameless lust and adultery, is the same Jesus who extended mercy to the woman caught in the very act. The Jesus who welcomed sinners in repentance is the same Jesus who prophesied against those who would not repent.

When we talk about love and law, then, we are not talking about two different things that must balance each other out. When we talk about law and love, we are talking about the depth and fullness of God's character: a character we are intended to reflect in all its complexity. As we are changed into His image, we will necessarily mature in our own capacity to love and be forced beyond simplistic categories and legalistic rules.

This is why those who opt for overly simplified understanding of either law or love often seem half-human or one-dimensional. They are existing in only one dimension of God's character. Those who rely on legalistic rules as a way to gain God's love miss that He already loves them. And those who insist that God's love transcend His rules miss that those very rules were given *because He loves them.* In this sense, legalism and sentimentality are branches of the same tree; at root, they are attempts to find identity—to love—apart from God.

Transformed by His Love

Ultimately, the only way to find identity *imago dei* is to have our hearts shaped after God's own heart. To love what He loves so we will do what He does. God did not intend for us to be actors performing roles but to be people living in intimate relationship with Him and others. This happens as our hearts are changed by His love and then kept desiring the right things by dependent union with Him through prayer, meditation, personal study, and communion with others. Through these spiritual graces, our hearts are shaped after His and we are then able to desire the right things. And when we desire the right things, we will do the right things.

We will finally be the image bearers we were meant to be.

And this is precisely what the apostle John promises will happen; God's ever-present love for us today will transform us into people who love like Him tomorrow. His love will make us who we really are. In 1 John 3:1–2, he writes:

> See what kind of love the Father has given to us, that we should be called children of God; and so we are. . . . Beloved, we are God's children now, and what we will be has not yet appeared; but we know that when he appears we shall be like him, because we shall see him as he is.

chapter 6

Good Gracious Me:
Cultivating a Large, Generous Soul

*"Grace is but glory begun, and glory is but grace
perfected."—Jonathan Edwards*

"**M**ommy, did you know that baobab trees swell up like balloons because their trunks fill with water?"

My daughter is at the stage of childhood where life is one big treasure hunt—a world just waiting to be explored. She regularly stays up past bedtime with her nose in a book only to greet us the next morning, sleepy-eyed but eager to share some fact she has recently discovered.

But her discoveries aren't limited to horticulture, and they aren't limited to books or the classroom. Recently we've realized that recess can expand her vocabulary as quickly as language arts ever could. Fortunately the third graders in our community still exist in a sphere of childhood where they have a reverence for mouths washed out with soap and have yet to develop the *chutzpah* to actually say certain words without encoding them as "the A word," "the B word," and "the D word."

The only problem with this secret code—this linguistic gnosticism—is that it sparks the curiosity of kids who aren't privy to the actual words themselves. Kids like my daughter. But because I'd rather that she learn them from me, we have a standing agreement that whenever she wants to know what a particular word means, she can come to me without condemnation or judgment and ask. And I will do my best to tell her the truth and not freak out in the process.

So one day, when she came to me wanting to know about "the B word," I breathed a heavy sigh and, in as calm and collected way as possible, told her the truth. In a situation like this, I begin with an extensive foray into etymology and literal meaning, I explore the difference between connotative and denotative language, and yes, I stall in the off chance that I might bore her to the point that she'll lose interest and I won't actually have to tell her the more vulgar meaning.

It rarely works.

So this time, I ended up telling her that "the B word" originally meant nothing more than a female dog and that over time, it came to mean a woman who is mean, spiteful, or contemptible. In essence, a woman who lacks grace. Eventually "the B word" devolved even further and is now used in a way that is so demeaning and so pejorative that we consider it profane. In short, it's a bad word; don't use it.

Still, being a person who could never pass up a good etymology, it struck me that "the B word" was originally used to describe an animal. In essence, we are saying that a woman who acts this way—a woman who is mean, spiteful, contemptible—is not behaving like a woman at all. She is behaving like an animal. Even if we don't have the theology to express it or to even understand why it's problematic, we instinctively know that a woman who lacks grace is not existing as she was made to exist. A woman who lacks grace is not existing *imago dei*.

People of Grace

"For grace proclaims the awesome truth that all is gift.
All that is good is ours, not by right, but by the sheer bounty
of a gracious God."—Brennan Manning

In the last chapter, we explored how being an image bearer means becoming a person who loves properly. When your heart is fixed on God as the source of your identity, your desires and affections align with His and enable you to live as you were meant to live: in dependent relationship with Him, in communion with others, and as a proper steward of the earth. But this same love is so powerful, so abundant, so life-giving, that it also makes us gracious people who reflect the grace and generosity of God Himself. As the old adage goes, "You can give without loving, but you cannot love without giving." In recent years, the idea of grace has experienced something of a comeback in the church. But while it has become very popular to talk about grace, I'm not convinced that we always understand what we're talking about. We know that grace is an essential theme of Scripture—something so powerful and necessary to Christianity that we cannot even discuss our faith without it. In fact, we know it is so powerful that we'll even enlist it as a weapon in our theological debates, simultaneously and ironically accusing one another of "misunderstanding grace."

Most often, though, we use grace as a synonym for God's forgiveness and our inability to earn our salvation.[1] "For by grace you have been saved," after all, "and this is not of your own doing . . . not a result of works."[2] But because we think of grace primarily as God's forgiveness, we also tend to think of grace as a *response*. But

---

1. In its basic form, the Greek word for grace (*charis*) means "favor or kindness." It also includes the idea of "inclining toward" or extending yourself toward someone (http://biblesuite.com/greek/5485.htm).
2. Ephesians 2:8–9.

grace is not simply God's response to our sin; grace is the essential nature of a God who is already intentionally inclining Himself toward you. In this sense, forgiveness is the *result* of a grace that already exists; it is the fruit of a tree whose roots run deep, ever reaching, ever stretching, further and further into the generous nature of God Himself.

God is, in fact, so abundantly and essentially generous that even His identity cannot be contained and comes spilling out, overflowing to us as His children. The very concept of *imago dei* is rooted in grace because God is *sharing* His identity with us. This is not a god who restricts himself or holds back, aloof like the gods of the ancients. He is a God who gives and gives and gives and gives some more.[3]

And the greatest gift that He gives is Himself.

Full of Grace and Truth

When Jesus came to earth, the Scripture says that He "became flesh and dwelt among us, and we have seen his glory, glory as of the only Son from the Father, full of *grace* and truth . . . and from his fullness, we have all received, *grace upon grace.*"[4]

Grace upon grace. Gift upon gift.

Because God is essentially generous, Jesus as the perfect Image Bearer embodied this same generosity. It was not enough for Him to get to Galilee; He "had" to go through Samaria to meet the woman at the well.[5] As the Good Shepherd, He doesn't wait for His lost sheep to return to the fold but actively seeks us out. And the night before the cross, He took bread and wine and said, "This is my body, which is *given* for you."[6]

---

3. James 1:17.
4. John 1:14–16.
5. John 4:4.
6. Luke 22:19.

Never before was grace so clearly seen, so clearly demonstrated than in Jesus Christ.

When you remember that *imago dei* identity is defined by relationship, you can begin to understand how grace—the inclining of yourself toward another person—strengthens and maintains the bonds between us. And you also begin to understand why the forgiveness that flows from grace is essential to becoming the people God created us to be.

Because we were made to live in relationship, when the bond between us and God was severed through sin, we were unable to be who we were created to be. Our loss of self, the wandering, the isolation—all are the direct result of the fact that we are cut off from God and one another. So when Jesus Christ freely offered Himself, when He extended Himself to us—when He *graced* us with Himself—He restored the bond that was broken. Even the word "forgive" includes this fundamental idea of grace.

When God forgives us, He is *giving* Himself to us. Despite the fact that we have rejected Him, despite the pain we have caused, despite the brokenness, He is extending His favor and good will to us just as He extended it to us in those first moments of existence. Just as He extended Himself to us at the cross.

So it is only in the midst of this grace, in the midst of this divine grace upon grace, that we can finally know ourselves and find identity as image bearers. Not only because the bond between us and God has been restored, but because His grace can now flow *through* us, restoring the brokenness that separates us from each other. When He is alive in us, when our identity is joined to His, we become fundamentally gracious people. So by extending Himself to us, He enables us to extend ourselves to each other in the same way.[7]

---

7. Ephesians 4:32.

Gracious Living

*"By judging others we blind ourselves to our own evil
and to the grace which others are just as entitled to as we are."*
—*Dietrich Bonhoeffer*

I grew up in western Pennsylvania where Rust Belt poverty met Appalachia coal fields. My father's family had been farmers there for generations, but by the time I came along, ours was the second poorest county in the state. It hadn't always been this way. At one point in the early twentieth century, our county seat boasted the most millionaires per capita in the entire United States, and rumor has it that in the 1950s, there was a thriving gambling ring with ties to the New York and Chicago mobs. But over the subsequent years, the coal and steel markets restructured, the mines closed, and the population dwindled. Those who were left worked hard to care for their families and hold their heads high, but it wasn't easy, and more and more of the population slipped into generational poverty. And with it came a fear and worry, a sort of closing off, a battening down of the hatches, a preservation instinct.

One of the greatest challenges to living in *imago dei* grace is learning how to extend grace to those around you despite the brokenness of the world. In a world where we routinely hurt each other and where little is certain, being generous is risky business. So we refrain from giving; we hold back; we protect ourselves. And in the process, we become cynical, hopeless people who cannot believe in grace for ourselves because we refuse to offer it to others.

These fears often manifest themselves as tribalism and judgmentalism. For a society that prides itself on tolerance, we are also a society that fundamentally lacks grace when we interact with each other. You only have to read blog comments, listen to talk radio, or watch what happens when a scandal breaks—when some public figure makes a mistake or fails at his duties or says something inappropriate. If he's an ideological opponent, we quickly become rabid animals, gleefully watching his demise. If we are his supporters, we insist that he did nothing wrong, even as we know that he probably did.

And in either case, there is no forgiveness; there is no redemption. No public apology is sufficient. No attempt to pay back is enough. No acknowledgment of guilt or repentance will ever be adequate. And we wonder why the people closest to us—in our homes and churches and schools—have a hard time acknowledging their own failures. Could it be that we've faithfully demonstrated to them that there will be no grace when they do?

For all the damage that comes from removing prayer from schools, by treading on personal freedom, and by embracing sexual promiscuity, nothing could be more damaging to a society than walking away from grace. Because when we walk away from grace, we walk away from the only thing that has the power to heal our brokenness. When we walk away from grace, we walk away from the only thing that can restore the bonds of *imago dei* identity. When we walk away from grace, we walk away from the only thing that can make us human once again.

When we do not extend grace to those around us—when we hold ourselves back because of fear or pain—we are really restricting *ourselves* from being what we were meant to be. When we respond in anger and bitterness, it only furthers the divide between us as image bearers; and after the initial rush of adrenaline, we plummet into hollow, empty places. This is why people who hold grudges seem so small. They are not existing in the largess of God's grace; they are not existing in the fullness of His nature. They are not existing as image bearers.

Our God doesn't bear grudges. He doesn't hold Himself back to punish us. He doesn't "teach us a thing or two." Instead, in the face of unbelievable rejection, even as we turn from Him again and again, He patiently, generously, abundantly extends Himself to us. And when we finally return to Him, and to each other, He faithfully, freely forgives and makes us whole once again.

The Power of Grace

"Amazing Grace, how sweet the sound, that saved a wretch like me." —John Newton

The power of grace lies in its ability to make us fully human once again. But not only does grace make *us* fully human, it also has the power to make others fully human *through us*. When we extend grace to those who have harmed us, we are not only imaging God, but we are extending His nature to them as well.[8] We are extending to them the opportunity to live in their true identity. We are extending to them the possibility of redemption.

Victor Hugo captures this in his novel *Les Miserables.* The story takes place in early nineteenth-century France, a generation after the French Revolution. The main character, Jean Valjean, has been imprisoned for nineteen years for stealing bread and repeatedly attempting to escape. Those years were harsh and cruel, and the weight of judgment still hangs about him even after his release. Out on parole, Valjean is shunned by society, which propels him further toward hopelessness and ruin.

One night, after days of searching for work and shelter, an exhausted Valjean finds refuge at the home of Bishop Myriel, a Catholic priest. The bishop welcomes him in and even allows him to sleep in his own bed, but during the night, temptation proves

---

8. First Corinthians 7:14 teaches that a believing wife can be a sanctifying element in her unbelieving husband's life. The grace of God can flow into his life because it is flowing through her.

too much and Valjean steals the house silver and runs away. He is quickly caught and the authorities return him to the bishop for questioning.

To Valjean's surprise, the bishop doesn't condemn him but insists that he "gave" the silver to Valjean and to prove his point, hands over two more silver candlesticks. Once the authorities leave, Bishop Myriel urges Valjean to use the silver to become an honest man. He tells him, "My brother: you no longer belong to evil, but to good. It is your soul that I am buying for you. I withdraw it from dark thoughts and from the spirit of perdition, and I give it to God!"

The bishop's gift wasn't as much the silver as the grace that he extended; and this grace begins a process of transformation through which Valjean can finally begin to see the potential of his life. He can finally see his true identity as a person devoted to God and his fellow man. The transformation is not immediate, but it begins with grace.

One of the most powerful things about grace is that it gives us a vision for who we could be.[9] In the midst of our brokenness, it gives us hope. When God extends Himself to us, He is not so much expressing a belief in our ability to change, but in His ability to change us. He is confirming that we are not beyond redemption; we are not lost causes. If He was willing to sacrifice Himself for us, He must have a plan to make us more than we presently are. He must have a plan to bring us to glory.

And when we as His image bearers extend grace to other image bearers, we are assuring them that this is true for them as well. We are telling them we believe that they are more than their sin. We are confirming that their lives are intrinsically valuable to God and that they, too, are destined for glory with us. By becoming

---

9. Titus 2:11–12.

gracious people, by living in *imago dei* grace, we mirror the hope of the gospel itself.

Grace and Glory

"For the Lord God is a sun and shield: the Lord will give grace and glory."—Psalm 84:11(KJV)

And it is this hope—the hope that God will continue to be just as generous as He has always been—that frees us to live with open hearts and open hands. It is this hope—the hope that His mercies are new every morning[10]—that allows us to rise up each day to live in the fullness of Christ. To live in "grace upon grace."

Because in order to be who you were intended to be, in order to know yourself and find identity as a image bearer, you must become a person whose very identity overflows in abundance toward those around you. You must become a person with a large soul who images your generous God. And as you rely on Him, He promises you will be able to do precisely this.

He promises "to bless you abundantly, so that in all things at all times, having all that you need, you will abound in every good work."[11] As you rely on His very grace to be gracious, He, who did not spare His own Son, "will also, along with him, graciously give us all things."[12] And when He does, you will be able to extend this same grace to those around you; and you will be able to watch as they are transformed by it. Just as you have been.

---

10. Lamentations 3:22–23.
11. 2 Corinthians 9:8 (NIV).
12. Romans 8:32 (NIV).

chapter 7

Lady Wisdom:
Thinking God's Thoughts after Him

"May the mind of Christ my Savior / Live in me from day to day / By his power and love controlling / All I do and say." —Kate Wilkinson

I attended a Christian liberal arts college, and during my junior year, I took one of the most sought-after courses on campus: Philosophy of Education.

It was taught by a gruff German professor (aptly named) Dr. Guenter Salter, who, among other things, assumed that if he had perfected English grammar, we as native speakers would be held to the same standard. He would not give full credit for an answer unless it was spelled correctly and used in a grammatically correct sentence. A rumor circulated that he interviewed potential graduate assistants by grilling them on the proper use of "lie" and "lay."

Still, I was eager for this class because I had grown up in a home that valued learning. My father's mother, Stella, was the first in her family to graduate from high school by walking the three miles from her family farm to the high school in their small mountain community. At sixteen, my maternal grandmother, Ruth, traveled over seven hundred miles away from home to become the first in her family to attend college; while there, she met my grandfather, who was also the first in his family to attend college, due in large part to the GI Bill.

So it wasn't too surprising that my parents both ended up as teachers, and I grew up with more books than toys. I remember the year my parents bought a *Funk & Wagnalls* Encyclopedia. (I say "year" because despite a meager income, they faithfully bought one volume a week when Shop 'n Save used it as a loss leader to draw customers.) While other moms brought home glassware, mine brought home books.

Settling in for that first session, I was ready for Dr. Salter to inspire me with the beauty and wonder of learning; more than anything I expected him to shore up my own presuppositions. What I wasn't prepared for was for him to turn them completely on their head.

About halfway through that first class, Dr. Salter said something that sticks with me to this day. He challenged us that the goal of all learning is to become fully human—so far, so good—but then he went further. Because education is the process of making us fully human, true education must, by definition, be Christian because becoming fully human means being conformed to the image of God through Christ.

In a word, education is about finding identity as image bearers.

God of All Knowledge

"When you see the work of an artist your mind burns to know how and why it was created. It is the same with the world. God planted in us the unspeakable longing to know the how and why of his great works."—Origen

In chapter 5, I suggested that to be human, to be an image bearer, is fundamentally to be a lover. Because God is love, your true self is found in what you love, and you end up pursuing what you love. So why am I now saying that becoming an image bearer—becoming who God made you to be—also involves pursuing knowledge?

The simplest answer is that learning shapes what we love. This is why Paul appeals to the Romans (12:1–2) to be "transformed by the renewal of your mind," and why Solomon talks about those who are "wise of heart"[1]—they are those whose hearts have gained wisdom, those who have learned to love properly. So in one sense, true education is the process of learning to love the right things, of learning to love what God loves so we can reflect what He is and what He does. And the very reason that our minds can affect our hearts in the first place is because God is a thinking God. His love and His reason are inextricably bound together; and as His image bearers, love and reason are inextricably bound together in us as well.

From the earliest moments of creation, God reveals Himself as a God of knowledge. Jeremiah 10:12 proclaims that He "established the world by his wisdom, and by his understanding stretched out the heavens." Moses warns that "the secret things belong to the Lord"[2] and Isaiah says that God's thoughts are higher than ours.[3] This is also why Solomon says that "the fear of the Lord is the beginning of knowledge"[4] and Paul asserts that in Him "are hid all the treasures of wisdom and knowledge."[5] But God is not simply the starting place for wisdom; He *is* Wisdom, He *is* Truth Himself. And this was never clearer than when Jesus was revealed as the *Logos* of God.

---

1. Proverbs 10:8.
2. Deuteronomy 29:29.
3. Isaiah 55:8–9.
4. Proverbs 1:7.
5. Colossians 2:3.

Jesus the *Logos*

We've already seen that John identifies Jesus as "the Word." In the first sentence of his gospel, he writes, "In the beginning was the Word and the Word was with God and the Word was God." The English "word" is actually the Greek *logos*, so this verse could also read like this: "In the beginning was the *Logos* and the *Logos* was with God and the *Logos* was God."

Throughout history, translators have struggled to find just the right English word to translate *logos*. Because of this, sometimes they simply transliterate it—meaning they use the Greek word itself instead of an English word. In fact, we use *logos* regularly: words like biology, geology, theology, and anthropology all borrow from *logos* to convey the idea of "study of" or "learning."

But when translators encounter *logos* in Scripture, they don't transliterate it. Instead they use the English "word." But this translation has its limitations because "word" doesn't communicate all that *logos* means. When we use *logos* in the vernacular, it means "study" or "learning"; it includes the *idea* behind the word. In fact, we really can't separate words and ideas at all. If you are struggling to communicate a thought clearly, the problem isn't that you simply "haven't found the right words yet" but that your thoughts are not completely formed yet. In this sense, *logos* means both the expression of an idea (the word) and the thought that initiated it. So when John chooses to identify Jesus as the *Logos*, he is telling us that Jesus is the perfect embodiment of God's thought. Jesus is God's Wisdom made flesh, dwelling among us.

The beauty of this becomes breathtakingly clear when we remember what happened in Eden. As image bearers, our first parents were made to find their true selves in God who is perfect Truth; but instead, they turned from Him to the tree of the *knowledge* of good and evil. They turned away from true knowledge and were plunged into blind ignorance. Professing themselves to be wise, they became fools.[6]

So when John identifies Jesus as the *Logos* of God, he identifies Him as the true knowledge that we all have rejected. He is highlighting the fact that Jesus is quite literally "the way, and the *truth*, and the life."[7] What the man and woman lost when they grasped for knowledge apart from God—what we each lose every time we turn to something other than Him for our sense of self—Jesus restores by becoming the perfect thought, the perfect wisdom, the perfect knowledge of God in human flesh.

And it is from this *Logos*—from the very mind of God Himself—that all knowledge flows. And it is through this *Logos*—through the very person of God Himself—that we pursue knowledge in order to image Him.

All Truth Is God's Truth

"Nay, but let every good and true Christian understand that wherever truth may be found, it belongs to his Master."—St. Augustine

Looking back, I realize one reason Dr. Salter's words surprised me was because I had a disconnect between wisdom and knowledge. For me, wisdom was what you discover by reading the Bible and attending church; knowledge was whatever else you learn that may be interesting but has little bearing on your relationship to God and others.

And yet Scripture does not differentiate between sacred wisdom and secular knowledge. In Psalm 19:1, David sings that even "the heavens declare the glory of God, and the sky above proclaims His handiwork." Everything you could possibly learn—

6. Romans 1:22.
7. John 14:6.

from the physics that enable a suspension bridge to straddle San Francisco Bay to the social habits of whales to the tenderness of a mother's touch—everything reveals the majesty of the God "who established the world by His wisdom."[8] As Gerald Manly Hopkins expressed in "Pied Beauty," God gloriously reveals Himself in "dappled things . . . skies of couple-colour as a brinded cow . . . [and] finches' wings."

Because of this, *imago dei* knowledge is by necessity more than a dry, crusty intellectualism; it is more than a "worldview." At its root, *imago dei* knowledge is the capacity to wonder—to look for God's fingerprints everywhere and then to stand in awe when you finally see Him. *Imago dei* knowledge means searching for Him with childlike curiosity, wide-eyed and eager to discover who He is and the world He has made.

Arthur Holmes captured something of this when he said, "All truth is God's truth."[9] All that is true, all that can be known, belongs to God because God is the source of all Truth. Still, even as we understand that "all truth is God's truth," we also recognize that we are only able to *discern* what is true through the filter of His Word. The second half of Psalm 19—the same psalm that celebrates nature's ability to reveal God—also celebrates the power of God's law to reveal truth to us. "The *testimony* of the Lord is sure, making wise the simple . . ." David declares. "The *commandment* of the Lord is pure, enlightening the eyes."[10]

Because even though Scripture does not differentiate between sacred and secular fields of knowledge, it does differentiate between knowledge that humbly submits to God and false knowl-

---

8. Jeremiah 10:12.

9. Arthur F. Holmes, *All Truth Is God's Truth* (Grand Rapids, MI: Eerdmans, 1977).

10. Psalm 19:7–8; Theologians differentiate between "natural" revelation, the revelation of God's nature by general or universal means, and "direct" revelation, the specific revelation of God's nature through His Word.

edge that elevates man as the source of truth.[11] Paul describes the latter in 2 Timothy when he says that there are those who are "always learning and never able to arrive at a knowledge of the truth."[12] They cannot come to understand truth—they can never be who they are destined to be—because they have already rejected the One who is Truth Himself.[13]

But in His kindness, God reveals Himself to those who have eyes to see. To those who know Him as the source of all Truth, He reveals Himself in the cool mist that hovers on the mountainside; to those who listen, He reveals Himself in the quiet hymns sung at evening prayer; to those who study, He reveals Himself in the pages of His Word; and He will continue to reveal Himself, until with William Blake, you are finally able

> To see a World in a Grain of Sand
> And a Heaven in a Wild Flower,
> Hold Infinity in the palm of your hand
> And Eternity in an hour.[14]

Women's Work

"Well, knowledge is a fine thing, and mother Eve thought so; but she smarted so severely for hers, that most of her daughters have been afraid of it since."—Abigail Adams

One of my favorite literary heroines is Lucy Maud Montgomery's Anne Shirley of *Anne of Green Gables*. Anne is that spunky kind

---

11. 1 Timothy 6:20.
12. 2 Timothy 3:7. In this sense, even studying theology can be done in a way that actually leads us away from God and back to ourselves.
13. In 1 Corinthians 1–2, God's Wisdom is contrasted with worldly wisdom that rejects Him as the source of Truth.
14. From "Auguries of Innocence" by William Blake.

of girl who can never quite find her place in the world and is often too smart for her own good. In the opening scenes of Kevin Sullivan's 1985 film adaptation, we meet Anne walking through the woods with her nose in a volume of Tennyson. Lost in another world, she returns late to the Hammond homestead where she is working as a servant.

An already irritated Mrs. Hammond becomes livid when she discovers Anne's book and exclaims, "Well! If you paid more attention to your chores than poring over them fool books of yours . . ." She throws the offending book into the woodstove declaring, "If I catch you reading any more of those books of yours while you're supposed to be lookin' after my young'ns, they'll feed the fire too, missy!"

This scene sets up one of the key plot functions of the story and encapsulates what has been a tension for many women throughout history; when it comes to learning and education, a woman's place is in the kitchen, not the academy.[15]

Interestingly, Luke 10 records a similar encounter between two women during Jesus' earthly ministry. But instead of minimizing the importance of learning, this account strikes at the heart of the "don't bother your pretty little head" mentality that can sometimes be directed toward us. A mentality that we sometimes adopt for ourselves.

The story opens as Jesus is teaching in the home of the sisters Mary and Martha. As was typical, His disciples were surrounding Him, hanging on His every word; but on this particular day, Mary was among those sitting at His feet. In first-century Judaism, this

---

15. We must not take for granted the educational freedom that women have in modern Western society. This has not been the norm for most of human history, although Christianity has sought to educate women and many of the first schools for girls were church-based. On a worldwide scale, girls and women still trail behind their male counterparts in their opportunities for education.

would have been unusual for a woman because sitting at Jesus' feet indicated that she was learning from Him the same way that a student learns from a teacher.

In the background, Martha buzzed about, trying to fulfill her role as hostess, trying to feed all the extra hungry stomachs, trying to do what she knew to do. At some point she became frustrated and came to Jesus. "Don't you care that my sister has left me to serve alone?" she said. "Tell her then to help me." In Martha's mind, Mary should have been serving not learning. That's what women do after all, right? We're the nurturers, we're the hostesses, we're the caregivers. Mary needed to be in the kitchen, not at Jesus' feet.

But Jesus said something surprising. "Martha, Martha," He said, "you are anxious and troubled about many things, but one thing is necessary. Mary has chosen the good portion which will not be taken away from her."

The good portion.

And with these words, Jesus turned the idea of "women's work" upside down. For Him, the greatest work Mary could do that day was to sit at His feet and learn from Him. The greatest work she could do was to become like her teacher—the *Logos* Himself.[16] The greatest work she could do was to become an image bearer who reflected His knowledge.

Even today, there are those who question whether or not a woman should pursue education. They reason that women are primarily nurturers and life-givers, and they falsely believe that this doesn't require anything beyond learning a domestic skill set.[17] In response, others argue that certainly women must be educated but *precisely* because they are the mothers of society. They

---

16. Matthew 10:24–25.
17. My intent is not to diminish the *imago dei* thought and intention necessary to manage a home but to highlight the false paradigm that some make between domesticity and education.

104 | made for more

must be prepared to shape their children, to teach them well, and present them as mature, capable members of the church and society. Then, of course, some reject both of these approaches and stridently argue that women must be educated to free them from the shackles of domesticity. They must be educated in order to take their place on a rung of the corporate ladder.

As different as these approaches appear, they have something in common: all three presume that education is primarily about a career. Whether that career is motherhood or being a CFO, they are all based on the assumption that education is primarily about providing a skill set for future work. But what if education—what if learning and thinking and knowing—is less about what you *do* with your knowledge than it is about the person you become in the process? What if learning is less about how to make a living and more about how to live?

What if education is first and foremost about becoming image bearers?

When Jesus approved of Mary sitting at His feet, He invited all women to do the same. And here, all that Eve lost when she was deceived and fell into ignorance, He redeems by enabling us to become women who can open our mouths "with wisdom" (Proverbs 31:26). In the end, we pursue learning because God is a God of knowledge and thought and wisdom and in order to reflect and represent Him, we must become women of knowledge and thought and wisdom. This can take a variety of forms depending on context and personal giftedness, and it may not necessarily include advanced degrees or groundbreaking theories; but at the very least, becoming women who image Him, becoming all that we are created to be, means learning to love Him, not simply with all of our hearts, but with all of our minds as well.[18]

Pink Passages

"Study to shew thyself approved." —*2 Timothy 2:15 (KJV)*

This truth has startling implications for how we study Scripture. Too often as women, we have restricted ourselves to the "pink" parts of the Bible. When we identify first and foremost as women, we can begin to believe that knowledge of ourselves will come primarily through passages that speak to women's issues or include heroines like Ruth or Esther. But when we do this, when we craft our learning and discipleship programs around being "women," we make womanhood the central focus of our pursuit of knowledge instead of Christ.

And we forget that these "pink passages" were never intended to be sufficient by themselves. We forget that we can never understand what it means to be women of good works until we first learn about the goodness of a God who works on our behalf. We forget that nothing about them will make any sense if they are not first grounded in the truth that we are destined to be conformed to His image through Christ.

Because you are an image bearer, you must allow the entirety of Scripture to shape your sense of self. You must begin to see every verse as a "pink" passage because every verse speaks to who God is and therefore who you are as His daughter.[19] You must begin to believe that theology and doctrine are not men's issues but that they are *imago dei* issues because they reveal the God in whose image you are made.[20]

---

19. Certainly there are texts that we identify with as women, but we must be certain to ground these passages in the full orb of Scripture. If we don't, we will walk away from them with a checklist by which to evaluate our womanhood, rather than an understanding of how the gospel enters into our womanhood and transforms it.

20. I believe that part of this disconnect lies in the fact that we expect doctrine and theology to be expressed in a masculine way. Certainly we don't want to create "men's doctrine" and "woman's doctrine," but I wonder if we need to make room for feminine voices that can speak and write about doctrine and theology without having to adopt a masculine style to be heard.

And when you do this, when you pursue knowledge of Christ, the *Logos* of God, you will be transformed from the inside out. You will adorn what Peter calls the "hidden person of the heart,"[21] which will naturally express itself in your womanhood as quickly as it will into every other facet of your life—from your unique personality to your closest relationships to the work He has called you to do.

The Mind of Christ

"The last function of reason is to recognize that there are an infinity of things which surpass it." —Blaise Pascal

Ultimately the goal of all learning is to draw us back to humble dependence on the source of knowledge, God Himself; this in turn enables us to love one another more fully and exercise better care over creation. And yet, as quickly as we embrace our identity as learning image bearers, we can just as quickly be tempted to look to knowledge itself for our identity. And when we do, we will develop that bobblehead persona and for all our knowledge remain unchanged.

But true knowledge—knowledge that beings and ends with God—will humble us because when we finally begin to understand who God is, we will begin to realize how much we don't understand in the first place. When we finally see Christ as the Perfect Wisdom, we will begin to realize how much wisdom we lack.

And yet, in His grace, God promises that even though we may only know in part today, there will be a day when we will know

---

21. In 1 Peter 3:4, Peter calls women to specific applications but does so on the basis of their imaging Christ and having been transformed by Him. The applications to womanhood are the result of inner transformation of the heart, not the source of transformation itself.

Him as we have been fully known.[22] One day, we will finally be able to comprehend "what is the breadth and length and height and depth, and to know the love of Christ that surpasses knowledge."[23] When we do, Scripture promises that we will be filled with all the fullness of God. And when we know Him this way, when we *know* the love of Christ both mentally and experientially, we will finally be transformed into the image bearers He has destined us to be.

---

22. 1 Corinthians 13:12.
23. Ephesians 3:18–19.

chapter 8

Queens in Narnia:
Embracing Your Destiny to Reign

*"Work is the natural exercise and function of man—the
creature who is made in the image of his Creator."*
—Dorothy L. Sayers

"Once upon a time . . ."

For centuries, these words have unlocked a world of imagination and wonder, inviting us to a place where bears talk, awkward cygnets transform into graceful swans, and poor boys stumble into riches. What could never exist here suddenly becomes the standard of reality there; and all it takes to dispel sadness and ensure that good triumphs is a twirl of a fairy godmother's wand or a kiss from your one true love.

Understandably, fairy-tale princesses, with their turreted castles and strapping knights, have captured the imaginations of countless little girls long before Disney ever thought to enshrine them in Pantone pink No. 241. When my own daughter began her princess stage, I held my breath and tried to remember what these picture-perfect royals could teach her. Cinderella taught her to be joyful even in the face of injustice. Belle taught her that a good book is always a better companion than an arrogant man. And

Snow White taught her to be wary of strangers (unless of course, they happen to be three-foot-tall men, in which case, you should straighten their house and make them dinner).

Still, there was something I could never figure out. What exactly does a princess *do*?

In most stories, the actual work of being a princess is left fairly undefined; even worse, becoming a princess can mean that you can escape work altogether. When Prince Charming finally finds Cinderella, he whisks her off to the castle, away from her mop and dishrag, straight into a bevy of waiting servants. You might begin to think that the greatest threat to a princess doesn't come in the form of evil stepmothers or fire-breathing dragons, but in never finding purposeful, productive work. The greatest threat to a princess is that she might never grow up to be a queen.

Her Majesty, the Queen

C. S. Lewis captures the difference between a princess and a queen in his children's novel *The Lion, the Witch and the Wardrobe*. After Aslan has defeated the White Witch and restored peace to Narnia, he crowns the sisters Susan and Lucy as queens over the realm and commissions them to rule alongside their brothers, High King Peter and Edmund the Just. Lewis tells us that

> these two Kings and two Queens governed Narnia well, and long and happy was their reign. . . . they made good laws and kept the peace and saved good trees from being unnecessarily cut down. . . . and generally stopped busybodies and interferers and encouraged ordinary people who wanted to live and let live.

And with this slightly unconventional fairy-tale ending, Lewis affirms something that is true about the nature of every human being—something that is true about you. As God's image bearers, we may be royalty, but we are made to work.

Genesis 1 tells us that after God made mankind, He commissioned the man and woman to "be fruitful and multiply and fill the earth and subdue it and have dominion over the fish of the sea and over the birds of the heavens and over every living thing that moves on the earth."[1]

Later, David uses the same royal imagery when he says, "You have . . . crowned [mankind] with glory and honor. You have given him *dominion* over the works of your hands; you have put all things under his feet."[2] By entrusting us to care for creation, God reveals both how we would find identity and what that identity would propel us to do. Because we are made in His likeness, it is our destiny to rule and reign like He does.

But unlike kings and queens of the ancient world who ruled from lavish palaces, our God is a King who works. He is a King who rolls up His sleeves and gets down in the dust beside us. He is a King who makes Himself a servant and labors on our behalf.[3] In fact, the Scripture says this world is the very "work of His hands,"[4] and we ourselves are "His workmanship created in Christ Jesus."[5] So being an heir to this kind of King means that we are no fairy-tale princesses spending our days in idle luxury; we are queens ruling creation under His authority.

The very work we do—whether it is tallying numbers in columns of red or black, or scrubbing red and black crayon off newly painted walls—is an expression of God's royal nature in us. In this

---

1. Theologians often refer to these verses as the "Cultural Mandate;" God is commissioning His image bearers to represent Him by themselves creating and stewarding what He has made.
2. Psalm 8:5–6.
3. Philippians 2:5–7.
4. Psalm 8:6; also see Genesis 2:2.
5. Ephesians 2:10.

sense, just as education is about more than acquiring a skill set for a career, our work is about much more than acquiring a paycheck or professional honors. It is the very means by which we live out our *imago dei* identity; it is the way we become queens in Narnia.

Work in a Fallen World

Most of us do not think of our work this way. Work is simply what we must do to live. (And if you listen to my kids, you might begin to believe that work is an infernal punishment dreamed up by the likes of Dante himself.) The more we can escape it, the better. Part of this response is simply the result of experiencing work in a broken world. Originally, work was designed to empower the prismatic relationship that we have with God, with each other, and with creation. Through our work, we worship Him, serve the needs of others, and care for the world around us. But when the man and the woman turned from God as the source of their identity, they became something that they were never intended to be; and when they became something other than what God intended them to be, their work became something other than what God intended it to be as well.

Now, instead of empowering our relationships, our work can actually hinder them. All too quickly we look for our sense of identity from the work itself instead of from God. And lest we think this is only a temptation for those with careers, women who turn to their roles as wives and mothers for their sense of wholeness and identity can fall into the same trap. Further, we sometimes leverage our gifting and roles to oppress each other instead of serve each other; and too often, instead of stewarding creation, we pillage the natural world in order to consume its resources on our own lusts. Not only this, but the very act of work itself exists under a curse. Whether it is the work of bearing the next generation or of putting plow to field, our work—our very ability to rule and reign—has been made difficult, unrewarding, and futile.

So that instead of being kings and queens, we have become slaves.

Servant of All

"Come unto me all ye that labor and are heavy laden and I will give you rest... for my yoke is easy and my burden is light."
—*Jesus in Matthew 11:28, 30 (KJV)*

And yet. And yet, into this futility, into this brokenness, steps a Servant. A Laborer. A Worker. A Worker who comes to restore our ability to work *imago dei*. Philippians chapter 2 says that Jesus, "though he was in the form of God . . . emptied himself, taking the form of a servant . . . and being found in human form, he humbled himself by becoming obedient to the point of death, even death on a cross."

And by doing so, Jesus freed us from slavery and makes us people "zealous for good works."[6] No longer must we be relentlessly driven to find identity in our work. No longer must we use our work to one-up each other. No longer must we work out of obligation and duty. By *His* work on the cross, Jesus makes us people who can finally work as we are meant to. Because of Him, our labor is no longer in vain.[7]

But more than simply restoring our ability to steward creation, Jesus modeled what *imago dei* work will look like; He showed us in Mark 10:42–45 that being kings and queens means ruling through service:

---

6. Titus 2:14.
7. 1 Corinthians 15:58.

And Jesus called them to him and said to them, "You know that those who are considered rulers of the Gentiles lord it over them, and their great ones exercise authority over them. But it shall not be so among you. But whoever would be great among you must be your servant, and whoever would be first among you must be slave of all. *For even the Son of Man came not to be served but to serve, and to give his life as a ransom for many.*"

And with this, Jesus confirmed that being an image bearer means working for the good of those around you. Instead of being enslaved to our passions and fears, instead of jockeying for power and position, we fulfill our *imago dei* identity by serving—by using our gifts and capacities to honor Him and care for each other. Work becomes more than what we do to earn a living; it is one of the ways that we *live* in loving relationship with God and others. It is not a survival mechanism but the very means by which we flourish and enable others to flourish as well.

Stewarding Our Gifts

"Where your talents and the needs of the world cross; there lies your vocation."—Aristotle

Still, even if we understand that work means service, we could easily misapply this idea because we tend to have a specific mental picture of what a servant is. To us, a servant is someone who performs menial tasks enabling the upper classes to live in luxury. And while it is true that we must humble ourselves in order to serve well, serving each other through our work does not mean that we all rush out to become housemaids. It doesn't mean changing your work so much as changing *how* you do your work; it is not changing *what* you do but *why* you do it. Ultimately, working *imago dei* means using your God-given capacities and opportunities, not to serve your own interests, but to serve those around you.

Peter addresses this very idea in his first epistle. He writes, "As each has received a gift, use it to serve one another, as good stewards of God's varied grace: whoever speaks, as one who speaks oracles of God; whoever serves, as one who serves by the strength that God supplies—in order that in everything God may be glorified through Jesus Christ."[8]

Serving others through your work—being a queen that rules through service—means developing your unique gifts and leveraging them on behalf of others. These gifts include everything from our intellectual capacities to our artistic abilities to the biological ability to bear and nurture life.

In our culture, most of us hold one of two views of gifting and service. Either we think we can do whatever we want, and nothing and no one, not even our families, should stop us from achieving and fulfilling our personal goals; or conversely, we think that in order to truly be servants, we must suppress all our gifting and personal ambition. But both approaches miss a deeper truth: *your particular abilities are the very things that God has given you to serve others.* And you best image Him and serve others—not when you repress your passions and gifts—but when you cultivate and use them to serve others through His strength. Success isn't doing whatever you want to do; it is doing *whatever God has made you to do.*

In the New Testament, the church is described as an organic community of image bearers and is often likened to a body. Within this body, each member—each hand and foot and eye—must serve the others based on where God has sovereignly placed them.[9] They must do whatever God has created them to do. An

---

8. 1 Peter 4:10–11.
9. 1 Corinthians 12:18.

eye must be an eye; a hand must be a hand; a foot must be a foot. And the goal is that each would work effectively so the whole body can "build itself up in love"[10] through the different gifts that each member offers.

But this adds another layer to the conversation. Because *imago dei* work means serving each other through our unique gifts, we are then responsible to steward and develop those gifts. It is not enough to say that we *can* pursue our gifting; we *must* pursue our gifting. This is why Paul told his protégé Timothy to "fan into flame the gift"[11] that was in him. Timothy best served those around him by pursuing the talents and calling that God had already given him.

In the end, working *imago dei* means utilizing your God-given gifting and passion in order to strengthen your relationship with Him, with those around you, and as a steward over creation. It means surrendering to God's providence and embracing the calling He has given you—whether that means running after toddlers or running a Fortune 500 company. Or both at different seasons of life! Fulfilling your destiny as a queen over creation means humbling yourself like Christ and dedicating yourself to the work the Father has given you to do.

Home + Work

Another reason we struggle to understand *imago dei* work is because in Western society we tend to think of "work" primarily in terms of receiving a paycheck for a specific job. I remember being slapped in the face with this reality shortly after transitioning from being an ESL instructor to a stay-at-home mom. I was filling out one of those ubiquitous medical forms when I came to a field

---

10. Ephesians 4:16.
11. 2 Timothy 1:6.

that had the option to either fill in my employer's name or check a box that said "Don't Work." Having a strong commitment to intellectual honesty (and an even stronger philosophical disposition), I approached the receptionist to ask for clarification.

Instead she offered me a slightly puzzled look and then quickly replied, "Oh, you don't work."

Anyone who has been in a similar position understands how humbling, how demeaning this can feel. Whether you're a stay-at-home mom or have ever been unemployed or underemployed, you know how these situations strike at your core sense of self. Just think about the ingenious ways stay-at-home-moms describe their work in light of the marketplace by using terms like "domestic engineers" and "house managers." It's as if something about your very humanity is at stake, as if your identity as a productive human being is in question.

It feels this way because it is.

When we define "work" in terms of salary and position instead of in terms of gifting and service, we communicate that anyone who is not drawing a salary or working in the marketplace is somehow less human. And we end up elevating those who work in professional positions above those who work in more mundane callings.

This creates a unique tension for many women when they are forced to choose between being "at home" or "working." When the Industrial Revolution moved men and women away from family-based businesses to highly specialized jobs in cities and factories, as a society, we began to define "work" as whatever happened away from the home. (Insert joke about women who stay at home and eat bonbons and watch soap operas all day.) Frustratingly, the gender wars of the last several decades have only intensified this divide as both conservatives and progressives continue to argue about a woman's role in the "workforce." And as we do, we continue to define a woman's work by *where* she works instead of *in whose image* she works.

When God made us in His image, He commissioned men and women to rule over creation together. And not only are we to rule together, the very things that embody this rule—reproducing and stewarding the earth—must also be accomplished in dependence on each other. These are not two distinct commands but one command that exists with internal tension and intrinsic interconnectedness. In other words, God did not create the marketplace and the home to be in competition with each other but to depend on each other; and when we insist on pitting them against each other, we end up failing at both.[12]

As women, we must recognize that *imago dei* work is larger than either that of the home or the marketplace, both encompassing and transcending them. And as image bearers, we rule over both. We do not enslave ourselves to cultural expectations of domesticity but rule over domesticity, using it to cultivate a place where every member—every image bearer—can flourish. Neither are we slaves to the marketplace, conforming to mechanistic structures of input and output; instead we exercise our personal gifting, as Peter says, "to serve one another." We use our gifting to serve our families and those around us well.

A prime example of this is the woman described in Proverbs 31. When Lemuel's mother advises him about the type of woman he should marry, she describes a woman who would make his family successful because she works sacrificially and does "not eat the bread of idleness." She is the type of woman who knows

---

12. In July 2012, *The Atlantic* published a now famous article by Princeton professor Anne-Marie Slaughter entitled "Why Women Still Can't Have It All." In it, Slaughter argues that modern workplace dynamics force women to choose between work and home and as a result, employers lose some of their most valuable assets. Instead, Slaughter suggests that we need to completely overhaul how work and home intersect.

how to leverage the marketplace to care for her family, and at the same time receives public praise because she cares for the needs of others.[13] And yet, this passage is not some starry-eyed attempt to "have it all" but a beautiful description of finding the convergence, the delicate interplay, the holistic union of both nurturing our homes and exercising our unique gifting.

Undoubtedly there will be seasons of life when we must emphasize one over the other. (Quite frankly, there will be many times when you must weed your garden or change a dirty diaper or do something that will not directly capitalize on your MBA.) But we must stop assuming that our homes and our gifts are separate. Being women who work *imago dei* means being women who are productive and sacrificial wherever we are because our God is productive and sacrificial everywhere that He is.[14] Working *imago dei* means working like Him.

Queens Who Serve

And once we reach this place—once we realize that our work is defined by God—we can rule as queens over creation even if it means using a dust mop as a scepter. Because as lofty and as glorious as it sounds to rule and reign as God does, there will be many times that this will happen in less than "royal" ways. There will be many times we work more out of necessity than desire, and many, many times we will be tempted to think that certain types of work are beneath us.

---

13. Paul echoes a similar understanding of *imago dei* work when in both 1 Timothy and Titus he specifically warns women against idleness and instructs them to engage in work that actively blesses those around them.

14. In *Are Women Human?* Dorothy Sayers writes, "Every woman is a human being—one cannot repeat that too often—and a human being must have an occupation, if he or she is not to become a nuisance to the world." (Grand Rapids, MI: Eerdmans, 1971), 33.

This is precisely why we must base our understanding of work on who God is and what He has done. When Jesus stooped from glory to work for us; when He became a servant; when He girded Himself with a towel and washed His disciples' feet; He showed us that as His image bearers, nothing is beneath our dignity if it means serving Him and each other well.

Ultimately working *imago dei* means understanding that all work is sacred, all ground, holy; not because of what the task is *but because of who we are imaging*.[15] As you tackle your sink full of dishes, you are exercising dominion over the creation just as He does. As you serve lunch to rows and rows of hungry bellies in a school cafeteria, you are feeding them just like He feeds us. Piles of laundry, forms to be filed, and floors to be mopped are not barriers to self-fulfillment; they are opportunities to serve others the same way Christ serves us.

Martin Luther went so far as to say that it is God Himself working through us to care for His world in these "menial" tasks, that our vocations are "the masks of God" and that "God milks the cows through the milkmaid." In this way, through our work—whether it is a direct expression of our personal gifting or just the mundane things that must be done to make life function—we become the very hands and feet of God; we reflect and represent Him on this earth. And through our work, we become the image bearers we were made to be.

---

15. Sometimes, in response to those who dismiss mundane work as unimportant, we respond by elevating the task or specific calling. The danger of this is that it simply shifts the reference point from one type of work to another. Work is holy, not because of what it accomplishes or whether we value the result, but because of who it images—God Himself.

chapter 9

Toward Perfect Union:
Living Holistically in a Fractured World

"Among all things called one, the unity of the Divine
Trinity holds the first place."—Bernard of Clairvaux

When I was growing up, the decorating scheme of our home was decidedly eclectic.

This was due in part to a fire that ravaged our home the summer after I turned six. We were away on vacation at Myrtle Beach when my parents got a call telling them that our A-frame log house had been hit by lightning from a summer thunderstorm. When we returned, we recovered what we could, but smoke and water had damaged the furniture that survived. Thrifty as she was, my mom still found a way to salvage some of it, even if it meant throwing a tablecloth over a certain drop-leaf table when guests came over.

Despite our eclectic approach, one piece of furniture stands out in my memory—a cherry secretary desk that my mom inherited a few years after the fire. The front had four drawers with brass handles and it stood about four feet high. The real secret of this desk, however, was hidden behind the lid that dropped down to become the writing surface. Once opened, it revealed an array of cubbies, pigeonholes, and drawers. There was even a set of wooden columns that masked two secret compartments, which at the time I could only assume had been designed to hide secret papers of national consequence, coded maps, or the will of a long-lost relative that would ultimately restore our family's proper fortune.

I've since learned that ours was a modest desk in comparison to others. It didn't have a hutch on top; it wasn't an antique; and it didn't have much of a background story. Still, it served its purpose and all our important papers—from electric bills to field trip forms to birth certificates—eventually found a home in one of its nooks or crannies.

But as helpful as compartments were for organizing the paperwork of a busy family, they are not always helpful in pursuing *imago dei* identity. In fact, one of the biggest barriers to a flourishing life is our tendency to separate our identity into categories. We define ourselves by things like race, gender, and gifting, and inevitably end up elevating one of these categories above the others. Our first identity comes from being "an African-American" or "a woman" or "a writer."

Or if by chance, we avoid emphasizing one aspect of identity, we can easily end up thinking of ourselves as an odd assortment of unrelated characteristics—a collection of bits and bobs—rather than a whole person. This bit of life goes here, that part of us goes there; and none of it has anything to do with the other parts. But because we are image bearers, our identity is not simply the sum of our various parts. Because we are made in God's image, we are made to reflect His own wholeness and unity. We are made to live holistic lives.

"The Lord Is One"

*"If our love were but more simple, we should take Him
at His word; and our lives would be all sunshine in the sweetness
of our Lord."—Fredrick Faber*

For some, the word "holistic" conjures up an image of an aging hippie in a floor-length skirt, surrounded by swirling incense, humming to the low vibrations of a Tibetan singing bowl as she attempts to become "one" with the universe. For others, "holistic" simply means pursuing a lifestyle that flows naturally from work to school to home. It is a concept that affects everything from city planning to why your cousin suddenly quit her job and moved to the country to raise sheep and produce organic wool.

Or why you did yourself.

At its most basic level, a holistic life is an attempt to coordinate and integrate the various aspects of identity into one complete package. It is a search for internal peace and unity, and its absence can often be the very reason people begin searching for meaning and purpose in the first place. In fact, entire world religions are based on the promise of finding wholeness or *nirvana*. Even as Christians, we pursue an elusive "balance" and often believe that peace simply means finding the midpoint between two extremes.

But wholeness isn't simply about finding the middle ground, forgoing desire, or obliterating the different parts of your identity. And it's not about giving equal time and shared custody to the categories of life. Wholeness comes when the parts of your life work together because they have been united by something greater than themselves: when they have been united by God's own wholeness.

When theologians speak about the wholeness of God, they are referring to the fact that God's identity cannot be divided. Despite being three distinct persons, He is still one God. Despite being both Love and Righteousness, these "parts" of Him are not in opposition but work in splendid, peaceful coordination. In fact, for the theological purist, it is not even accurate to speak about "parts." God *is* Justice, God *is* Love, God *is* Truth, and God *is* Grace—all at the same time.

He simply is what He is.

Moses reminds the children of Israel of this in Deuteronomy 6 as part of his last words to them. After he reissues the Ten Commandments, he calls them to remember the unity and supremacy of Jehovah. While their pagan neighbors worship many different gods, assigning different attributes to each, Israel's God is one; He is all in all.

Moses cries out to them: "Hear, O Israel: The Lord our God, the Lord is one."

And then with his very next breath, Moses tells them that because their God is one, they must respond to Him holistically:

> You shall love the Lord your God with all your heart and with all your soul and with all your might. And these words that I command you today shall be on your heart. You shall teach them diligently to your children, and shall talk of them when you sit in your house, and when you walk by the way, and when you lie down, and when you rise.[1]

Not only are God's people to love Him exclusively, not having any other gods before Him, but we are to love Him with the fullness of our identities, to love Him with every aspect of our lives.[2]

---

1. Deuteronomy 6:4–7.
2. The wholeness and supremacy of God are intricately linked. Because God is One, all that can be thought of as Deity, all that should be worshiped as such, exists in Him alone. Paul echoes this in Colossians 2:9 when he writes that in Christ, "the whole fullness of deity dwells bodily."

And when we do, His nature will invade every nook and cranny of our being and we will experience His peace. We will exist in His *shalom*. The different parts of ourselves—all those things that seem to pull us in a hundred directions—will suddenly be unified because they are unified by God Himself.

Paul echoes this truth nearly fifteen hundred years later when he writes that Jesus came to "unite all things in him, things in heaven and things on earth . . . [and that] He Himself is our peace."[3] And then in his letter to the Colossians, he writes, "In Him all the fullness of God was pleased to dwell, and through him to *reconcile* to himself all things . . . making *peace* by the blood of his cross."[4]

As we submit every part of ourselves to Him, as He becomes the unifying element of our identity, we can finally achieve wholeness. We can finally be whole as He is whole. He does not obliterate the details of our lives, but pervades them in order to reconcile the different parts and make peace—in order to make them work together in beautiful coordination for our good and His glory.

Of Diamonds and People

"E pluribus Unum."—Great Seal of the United States[5]

Shortly after we were married, Nathan and I had the chance to travel through Western Europe. We started in Amsterdam and, despite the vestiges of jet lag, quickly found ourselves wandering up and down her streets, marveling at her canals, sampling fresh pastries, and devising ways to smuggle back home the bulbs we

---

3. Ephesians 1:10; 2:14.
4. Colossians 1:19–20.
5. This quotation means "out of many, one" and traces as far back as St. Augustine's use of *ex pluribus unum*, which he used to describe the Trinity.

had bought in the flower market. We felt contentedly European despite our obvious American ways.

While in Amsterdam, we also toured Gassan Diamond Factory where rough stones are cut, polished, and set into jewelry. We were the only ones on the tour, so our guide indulged our questions about everything from where diamonds come from to their own security measures. It seems that a diamond is naturally a fairly unassuming piece of rock, and only after diamantaires cut extra facets onto it does it begin to resemble what we think a diamond should look like. The more facets, the more brilliantly the diamond shines. In fact, a traditionally cut diamond has up to 57 different surfaces, and Gassan recently pioneered a technique that allows for an additional 64, making a grand total of 121! These facets capture light, reflect it internally, and then working in coordination, radiate it back so luminously that it appears as if the diamond itself were on fire.

In chapter 2, I suggested that *imago dei* identity is like a prism; it expresses itself through the three-dimensional relationship we have with God, with those around us, and as a steward over creation. When these three "planes" are properly aligned, God's nature shines through us, both illuminating our own lives and displaying the spectrum of His glory.

But in order to illustrate how Christ brings wholeness to your identity, I want to broaden the metaphor slightly. Instead of a three-planed prism, your identity is also like a multifaceted diamond. Because while living *imago dei* means loving God, loving others, and stewarding creation, this expresses itself in infinitely complex, infinitely individualistic ways depending on everything from your gender to your age to specific gifting. These "facets" of your identity are much like the surfaces of a diamond. God has painstakingly planned them and cut them so the light of His nature can bend and refract through you and come bursting forth in brilliant splendor.

The fact that I am a woman, that I am a mother, that I am a writer—even where I live—all work together to enable me to image God in a more complex, more brilliant way than if my identity were simply one-dimensional. So even as we strive for wholeness, we do not reach it by diminishing the multidimensional nature of our lives. We find it through the complexity of them. We find wholeness as each facet is cut to capture and reflect the radiance of Christ Himself.

Simple Complexity

"I've always felt that a person's intelligence is directly reflected by the number of conflicting points of view he can entertain simultaneously on the same topic."—Abigail Adams

If you look at a diagram of a cut diamond, you will notice that the facets are angled in such a way as to allow light to reflect off one and bounce to another. But in order for this to happen, the facets must be cut in opposition to each other. Just like the facets of your own life sometimes seem to be in opposition to each other. Just like the facets of God's own nature sometimes seem to be in opposition.

The fact that God exists in wholeness does not mean that He is simple or easy to understand. In fact, to our minds, God's nature is infinitely complicated; His very wholeness expresses itself in complex ways. And one of the most common ways that He does this is through opposition; He reveals Himself through paradox.

A paradox can be defined as a "seeming contradiction"—two truths that appear to conflict. For example, the Scripture teaches that we must pursue God; but it also teaches that we are like sheep who naturally stray. It teaches that God is infinitely loving and "not wishing that any should perish,"[6] but it also teaches that He is infinitely just and will "render to each one according to his works."[7] He is sovereign, but we must choose to obey Him.

And the list continues on and on.

But because our minds are limited, we tend to avoid these paradoxes. Instead of embracing both truths, we try to simplify them by pitting them against each other and emphasizing one to the loss of the other.[8] Then we devote entire branches of philosophy and theology to upholding whichever attribute of God we prefer.

But instead of seeing paradox as a contradiction, we must learn to see paradox as a two-sided truth, as two facets of a diamond working in tandem. Instead of simply rejecting the truths as incompatible, we must embrace them both. Because when we do— when we wrestle through the tension instead of bypassing it—we allow the paradox to do precisely what it is intended to do. It forces us to enter more deeply and more completely into *both* truths; it allows God's nature to radiate more brilliantly than it could through one facet alone.

In his book *Mood Tides*, Dr. Ronald Horton illustrates the power of paradox using the time that Jesus spoke of Himself as a grain of wheat falling into the ground and dying to produce new life. Horton writes, "The apparent contradiction was in the very nature of the truth itself . . . the idea that death must precede life is a startling truth, observable in nature but darkly mysterious as a universal principle."[9]

By using a paradox, Jesus was able to teach something deeper,

6. 2 Peter 3:9.
7. Romans 2:6.
8. I once knew a theology professor who described the ultimate paradox of how evil could exist if God is both loving and sovereign as the problem of trying to hold three watermelons in your arms. Even if you somehow manage to hold two, you will never be able to pick up the third without setting one of them down.
9. Ronald Horton, *Mood Tides* (Greenville, SC: BJU Press, 2008), 26.

something more profound than either truth alone could have. It's not simply that a seed dies. It's not simply that life comes from a seed. The deeper truth is that life comes from death. The deeper truth is that life comes from *His* death.

Living Paradox

"Man is one *person who can, however, be looked at from* two *sides."*—Anthony Hoekema

As an image bearer, you should not be surprised that your own identity is often complicated and more layered than you realize. Like God Himself, your own wholeness is regularly revealed through paradox. Certain things about your life seem to conflict and on the surface don't appear to work together. And perhaps the most fundamental of these is that you are both body and spirit. You are both material and immaterial at the same time.

When God created us, Genesis says that He formed us from the dust of the ground and breathed into us "the breath of life." At this moment, when physical and metaphysical met, mankind became a living soul. And yet we are not simply two halves stuck together. We exist in what Anthony Hoekema calls a "psychosomatic unity."[10] What happens in our spirits expresses itself through our bodies, and what we do in our bodies directly affects our spirits.

This is one reason why Paul warns the Corinthian believers to avoid sexual immorality. He argues that because both our bodies and spirits belong to Christ, when we engage in sexual immorality with one, we automatically engage in it with the other. There simply is no such thing as an exclusively "physical" act. This union of spirit and body is also why James says that it is not enough simply

10. Anthony A. Hoekema, *Created in God's Image* (Grand Rapids, MI: Eerdmans, 1986), 217.

to bless a brother or sister in need without caring for them physically (James 2:16). If we do not care for them as whole people, we are not caring for them at all.

When we fail to embrace both the spiritual and physical dimensions of identity, one of two things happens; either we become fixated on the material aspects of reality and reject anything that cannot be touched, tasted, handled, smelled, or heard. Or we slip into a gnosticism that views our spirits as somehow more eternal, more godlike, more "real" than our bodies.

For most Christians, the second pitfall is more likely (the simple fact that you are reading this book shows that you value spirituality). The danger comes when we elevate our spirits and, as a result, begin to disdain our bodies as somehow less significant. One way this tendency shows itself is when we reject the "ordinariness" of life. We can create an artificial divide between the "secular" and the "sacred" spheres and begin to emphasize those experiences that are more quantifiably "spiritual." Things like prayer, church commitment, Bible memorization, and even vocational ministry can easily be elevated above more mundane callings that relate to the care of our physical lives—things like medicine, food service, or housekeeping. And suddenly, we've stratified our faith and what should be the means of grace instead become badges of personal pride.

Paradoxically, this same gnosticism can lead just as quickly to license. Paul argues in 1 Corinthians 15:32 that if our bodies are not significant enough for God to raise them from the dead, we might as well "eat and drink, for tomorrow we die." If we believe our bodies are less significant than our spirits, if we view the body as nothing more than a container, then it doesn't much matter what we do with them. The only things that "truly" matter are the immaterial aspects of your identity—things like love, joy, and peace.

But our bodies are just as essential to identity as our spirits, if for no other reason than that they are the means by which we actualize love, joy, and peace. Our bodies enable us to do loving, joyful, peaceful things. They are the means by which we live *imago dei*. But ultimately, our bodies are essential to our *imago dei* identity because Christ's body was essential to His. When He incarnated Himself, He chose to exist in the paradox of being both spirit and flesh. And it was through His flesh that He lived a perfect life of obedience, and it was through His flesh that He made peace through His death on the cross.

And it was *His flesh* that God raised three days later.

As John Updike put it in "Seven Stanzas as Easter," the whole of Christianity rests on this fact: "the molecules reknit, the amino acids rekindle[d]." And because His body was raised, one day our bodies will also be raised. The promise of the resurrection is that "this perishable body must put on the imperishable, and this mortal body must put on immortality."[11] On that day when our bodies are raised incorruptible, even death itself will not be able to separate what God has once joined together.

Are Women Human?

Another closely related paradox of *imago dei* identity is the paradox of gender and personhood. In recent decades, there has been strident debate about the roles of men and women in society and the church. Some argue that because gender is a significant, but not primary, part of identity, women should find their place through their gifting rather than their womanhood. Others volley back that gender should lead where a woman's gifts are utilized and that they find fullest expression as nurturers.

But the problem with the whole conversation is that it tends to separate a woman into parts and pit them against each other.

---

11. 1 Corinthians 15:53.

And unintentionally, women are forced to choose between two very essential truths about themselves. The fact that I am a woman demands that in some ways my identity and roles will be different from a man's. Despite being equal image bearers, we are not the same. God even chooses to reveal aspects of His nature through my womanhood that could not be understood otherwise. So in this sense, gender itself is as much a gift—a grace—as intellect or personality could ever be.[12]

Conversely, my *imago dei* identity cannot be summed up by my womanhood alone. While being a woman is essential to my identity, I am not "simply" a woman. There is a part of me that transcends my gender, so in the end, regardless of how conservative we may be, we must all agree that a woman has more in common with a man than she does with a female cat!

The paradox of identity is that I am both a woman who is a person and a person who is a woman.

And this will never make sense until both my womanhood and my personhood are united in Jesus Christ. But when they are, when we submit our whole selves to Christ, we will finally be free to serve Him with both our bodies and spirit. By embracing the paradox, we discover, not two separate truths about ourselves, but the beautiful simplicity that unites both. We discover the simplicity that can only be found in Him—that can only be found in the One who can hold all things together.[13]

---

12. Hebrews 10:5 illustrates this truth when it teaches that Jesus accomplished the Father's will through *His body*.
13. Colossians 1:17.

United

"Is Christ divided?"—Paul the apostle

In many ways, pursuing *imago dei* simplicity is anything but simple. It requires more than reducing our personhood to manageable categories and roles. It requires more than achieving balance between the different parts of life. It requires submitting every part of who you are—whether it is your womanhood, your gifting, or your personality—to every part of who He is.

And when you do, when you look to Jesus, the perfect Image Bearer who exists in perfect wholeness, you will once again find your own. You will find peace. You will find harmony. And like a brilliantly cut diamond, you will shine as the glory of His nature reflects and radiates through the different facets of your life.

Until one day, all things whether in heaven or in earth—or in your very identity—are finally united in Him. And until that day, the God of peace, who is simplicity Himself, will "guard your hearts and your minds in Christ Jesus."[14] And this same God through His very Oneness will "sanctify you *completely* [so that] your *whole* spirit and soul and body be kept blameless at the coming of our Lord Jesus Christ. He who calls you is faithful; he will surely do it."[15]

---

14. Philippians 4:7.
15. 1 Thessalonians 5:23–24.

chapter 10

A Kind Providence:
When Jesus Leads You All the Way

"My whole life experiences are proof of the sovereignty of God and his direct interference in the lives of men. I cannot help believing what I believe. I would be a madman to believe anything else—the guiding hand of God!" —Dr. Martyn Lloyd-Jones

In our family, metaphysical epiphanies strike at the most unassuming moments.

Like when we're heading home from a less-than-stellar trip to the grocery store, having exhausted nearly a week's worth of patience in explaining why we didn't buy Lucky Charms and Jolly Ranchers and why it's not a good idea to twirl down the pasta aisle, arms outstretched. On this particular day, I was following an exterminator's van, trying to navigate through an unfamiliar section of town because our normal route was blocked, when my then eight-year-old daughter piped up from the backseat:

"Mommy . . ." (thoughtful pause) "I just wonder, Why am I me? Why don't I have somebody else's life? I mean, why can't I see different things or do different things? Why am I me?"

I snapped to attention. Forget the Lucky Charms and blocked streets, this was a teachable moment.

"That's such a good question," I said. "In fact, people ask themselves that question all the time. I mean, why am I a woman? Why am I driving home in my van? Why do I have three children? These are the kinds of questions that we all ask about our lives, and—"

"Not me, Mommy," my six-year-old son quickly interjected. "I never ask myself those questions. I like my life."

Like most epiphanies, this one was soon eclipsed by other things—namely, arriving home and racing to see who could turn on the television first. The moment lasted a bit longer for me because it came on the heels of a conversation that I'd had with Nathan the previous weekend. We were celebrating our anniversary and as is natural on that kind of occasion, we were talking over the years that had led us to that point. There we were in our early thirties, with three kids, living in yet another state, finally settling into our first house, and none of it could have been predicted that day we exchanged vows over a decade earlier.

And there's a part of you that can't help but wonder what would have happened if at any point you had taken a different route. If a particular street hadn't been blocked and you had simply taken the road you intended. This kind of backward longing is most tempting when things aren't as they should be—when you feel like you've lost yourself along the way—and you being to believe that maybe, just maybe, you were meant to be someone else after all. That who you are today was not who you were supposed to become. And even if you were, in these moments, you wish—like my daughter—you could be someone else entirely.

It's All in the Details

One of the greatest challenges to embracing *imago dei* identity is wrestling with the aspects of life that are beyond our control. It's easy to understand how our basic humanity flows from God, to understand that we love because He is love or that we work because He does. The difficulty comes when we try to apply those truths to our individual circumstances, when we must grapple with our specific identities. *I know I am made to love—but to love him? I know I am made to steward creation—but in* this *job?*

And all too quickly we understand why they say, "The devil is in the details."

The truth that few of us care to admit is that we have very little control over our identities. So much of what makes you an individual—your gender, the family you were born into, your gifting—was determined before you even had a chance to voice an opinion on the matter. And that's not to mention the myriad decisions that we make, believing we exercise our own will, only later to realize how heavily influenced we were by the moment or the people around us. Decisions like:

- The college you attended because your friends were going there—the college that affected your long-term career opportunities . . .

- The person you married so young, when you thought you knew enough about life and yourself to make a good choice only to realize later how little you knew about anything . . .

- The once-in-a-lifetime job you turned down to work for a nonprofit; the nonprofit that eventually left you disillusioned by internal politics and private failures . . .

It's not that we have no choice in the matter, and it's not even that our mistakes and failures don't affect us; it's just that we become so enamored with our own ability to shape our lives, to be whoever we want to be, that we forget that who we are in this moment is as much a *gift* as the day we first entered the world.

We forget that our lives—our identities—have been given to us by God.

So in order to make sense of who you are as an individual, you must return to the basic truth that began this whole search; you must return to the truth that all things come "from Him and through Him and to Him." That all things—even the details of your life—have been ordained by God[1] and given to allow you to image Him in a unique way. That something as simple as your personality has been designed to draw you into communion with Him, into relationship with others, and toward your specific calling—all in order to make you who you are supposed to be.

Fearfully and Wonderfully Made

And yet, even when we finally acknowledge our lack of control, we often simply swing to the opposite extreme. Life becomes an odd assortment of biological and social mechanisms with personal identity nothing more than the result of an existential Rube Goldberg contraption. One life event touches off another, which in turn touches off another until the marble that dropped into the bucket at the beginning finally triggers an explosion that rings a bell at the end. We view ourselves as the sum of our nature and nurture or some complicated mix of the two.

But Scripture offers a different picture of identity, one that began before you were even born. In Psalm 139, King David (him-

---

1. Matthew 10:29–31.

self once considered too small and young to be of any significance) speaks of a God who is not distant and unconcerned, but who sovereignly and lovingly invests Himself in our lives from their earliest moments. "You formed my inward parts," David sings. "You knitted me together in my mother's womb. I praise you, for I am fearfully and wonderfully made" (vv. 13–14).

Fearfully. Wonderfully. This is no accident of biology.

Everything about our bodies—from those size 10 feet to those too closely set eyes to those thighs that we all love to hate—everything about us was wonderfully and personally shaped by God's hand. Personally shaped to reflect His unique nature. Personally shaped to bring us into relationship with Him and communion with each other. Personally shaped to bring us to glory.

But it gets better. David continues, "In your book were written, every one of them, the days that were formed for me, when as yet there was none of them. How precious to me are your thoughts, O God! How vast is the sum of them!" (vv. 16–17). In the same breath that he assures us that God ordained our physical life, he assures us that God ordained the path it would take—*the One who made us is the One who guides who we become.*

This, in a word, is providence. Providence is the intricate combination of God's power and His love working together to bring about the best for His children—working together to make them exactly who they are meant to be. Paul defines providence as God's ability to bring all things "together for good for those who are called according to His purpose."[2] Or, to put it in a simple mathematical formula: God's power + God's love = God's providence. And it is this providence, this personal involvement at each juncture of your life, that makes you who you are today.[3]

---

2. Romans 8:28.
3. Proverbs 16:9.

But if this is true, what do we do with the things that we don't like about ourselves? What do we do with the very real evil and pain that mark us in ways we can never erase? What do we do with our brokenness?

God's Playthings?

A couple of years ago, I found myself engaging my daughter in yet another conversation far beyond my pay grade. She was swinging on our backyard swing—her baby-fine hair tossing in the wind and her legs pumping hard against the blue summer sky. She was quiet for a bit and then suddenly exclaimed, "I know, Mommy! Maybe the world is like a great big dollhouse. And people are God's dolls. Maybe we're just God's dolls!"

Given her limited experience with reality—which to that point, consisted primarily of family, church, and toys—this was a perfectly logical conclusion to reach. In trying to grasp the nuance of providence, she had settled on a view that strongly emphasized God's power, or what theologians call His "sovereignty." The only problem was that her narrow definition of sovereignty had effectively diminished her own personhood. Instead of seeing providence as the source of her unique *imago dei* identity, she had begun to think of herself as a doll, as an object.

She's not alone.

In March 2009, *Time* magazine included a theological trend in their annual list of "Ten Ideas Changing the World." Many young evangelicals, it seemed, were recovering an understanding of God's sovereignty, an understanding that had been central to the way their Reformed and Puritan forefathers had understood the world. Along with many others, I too benefited from this renewed emphasis and gained a fresh vision for God's power and overwhelming majesty. We've been reminded that all things are

THE DAILY EXTRA

Trivia

October was called Winmonath in ancient England. What does it mean?

a. month of Sundays

b. women's month

c. wine month

d. monarch's month

THE DAILY EXTRA

50 Years Ago . . .

1966's Top 10 Best-Selling Novels in the U.S.

1. *Valley of the Dolls* by Jacqueline Susann
2. *The Adventurers* by Harold Robbins
3. *The Secret of Santa Vittoria* by Robert Crichton
4. *Capable of Honor* by Allen Drury
5. *The Double Image* by Helen MacInnes
6. *The Fixer* by Bernard Malamud
7. *Tell No Man* by Adela Rogers St. Johns
8. *Tai-Pan* by James Clavell
9. *The Embezzler* by Louis Auchincloss
10. *All in the Family* by Edwin O'Connor

Cat: a pygmy lion who loves mice, hates dogs, and patronizes human beings.

—*Oliver Herford*

Monday
OCTOBER 24

United Nations Day
Labour Day (NZ)

from Him and to Him and unto Him, that all of history truly is *His* story. Our souls have swelled, our praises have deepened, and our provincialism and self-centeredness have gotten a well-deserved kick in the pants. But in the process, I think we've forgotten that God is not simply His sovereignty. And we are not simply His playthings.

The problem comes when we isolate His sovereignty from everything else that He reveals to be true about Himself. In this one-dimensional approach, He can quickly become a kind of cosmic bully, like a pagan god who uses our lives for His own benefit. And we end up dehumanized in the process because in order to embrace this kind of god—one who would glorify himself at his creatures' expense—we have to cauterize our own hearts against suffering and ultimately become callous to the pain of others as well. Whatever happens to them will simply be "God's will" for them.

But believing in God's providence does not mean simply believing in His sovereignty; it means believing as equally strongly in His infinite love.

The deeper magic is that while God has the power to do whatever He pleases,[4] it pleases Him to exercise His power on behalf of His children. While our good *is* found in seeking His glory, it is His glory to bring about our ultimate good.[5] This does not mean that He will always shield us from pain or that there won't be things that we want to change about ourselves. But it does mean that in them, He has an overarching purpose and through them, He Himself will care for us.[6]

---

4. Psalm 115:3.
5. Romans 9:23.
6. Isaiah 43:2.

Victim Mentality

"The only way to deal with an unfree world is to become so free that your very existence is an act of rebellion."—Albert Camus

Still, while a diminished view of His love can result in a diminished sense of self, a diminished view of His power can result in the exact the same thing. If we view God as too weak to guide our lives, we will become small, fearful people, tossed by fate, always reacting to other people's choices. Instead of being defined by power and love, we will become defined by fear, anger, and impotency. Some people respond to this sense of helplessness by recklessly indulging their every desire in order to achieve some level of control. By doing only what *they* choose, only what *they* want, they expect to free themselves, but instead, they can quickly become mastered by their own lust, anger, and fear.

None of which reflect God's character or allow us to live *imago dei.*

When we fail to embrace God's sovereignty in the details of our lives, we become victims. And nothing strips us of our humanity faster than becoming a victim, if only for the simple reason that God is not a victim. He is a God of power and love and wisdom, and as His image bearers, we must be women of power and love and wisdom as well.[7] In order to be who we were created to be, we must not only acknowledge the brokenness of this world, we must at the same time affirm that the love and power of God is stronger still.

Peter addresses the problem of suffering in his first epistle. While he acknowledges that some suffering is the result of our own foolish choices, he spends most of this letter speaking to those caught in situations beyond their control—bad work en-

---

7. 2 Timothy 1:7.

vironments, unjust authorities, difficult marriages. And yet, he doesn't offer condolences or platitudes; instead, Peter offers a vision of redeemed suffering, a vision of powerful, productive lives in the midst of the chaos. Lives so powerful that they could even affect the destiny of another person's soul.

In chapter 3, Peter speaks to the experience of a woman who has come to faith in Christ while her husband remains an unbeliever. Perhaps she embraced Christ after she and her husband were married; perhaps when they married, both she and her husband professed faith, but over the years, he rejected what he had once affirmed. Either way, behind the seemingly mild description of being married to a man who does not "obey the word" lies a world of suffering and confusion: the strain of trying to raise children together when your values differ, the loneliness of Sunday mornings when everyone else's family sits smiling together in the pew, and the fear that the one you love most in this world is facing a life apart from the One who is Life Himself.

But instead of counseling women to find a way out of these difficult marriages, Peter encourages them to image Christ's own suffering. He encourages them to "do good and do not fear anything that is frightening."[8] He encourages them to live with such strength and faith that the beauty of their lives would eventually win their husbands to Christ.[9]

The verses just prior to this illustration, 1 Peter 2:23, teach that this kind of powerful, fearless living is only possible when you entrust yourself to God—just like Jesus did when He suffered for us on the cross. Remember that Jesus did not suffer out of

---

8. 1 Peter 3:6.
9. We must recognize the difference between enduring a difficult marriage and enabling an abusive one. When a woman is caught in an abusive situation, her *imago dei* identity is under attack, and we must do everything in our power to defend and support her. Remember, Christ suffered from a place of power and love, not helplessness.

impotence; He was not a victim of circumstances. He was on a mission and He willfully submitted Himself to death because He knew He could trust the Father's providence. Because He believed His Father was ultimately in control, He knew that His suffering would not be in vain.

We often attribute this trust to Jesus' deity and His understanding of God's greater plan of redemption. And while this is true, it does not change the fact that we can believe and rest in *that very same plan.* We can rest in His plan to redeem the world. We can rest in His plan to reconcile us to Himself and each other. We can rest in His plan to make us who we were always meant to be.

And because we can, we also can rest in the truth that who we are, and the things that shape us are part of God's plan for our greater good. Because even when things about your identity don't make sense to you, they do make sense to Him. And so we entrust ourselves to Him who judges rightly—we entrust ourselves to His power and His goodness. And when we do, we are able to reflect this very same power and goodness in our own lives.

We are able to echo Jesus when He said that no one takes His life.[10] We are able to say, "You would have no authority over me at all unless it had been given you from above."[11] We are able to pray, "Your will be done."[12] And in these moments of surrender, we are never more powerful.

We are never more like Him.

Meant for Good

Another example of this kind of *imago dei* living—at least a more exclusively human one—is the Old Testament account of Joseph.

---

10. John 10:18.
11. John 19:11.
12. Matthew 6:10.

As the favorite son of his father, Joseph attracted the jealousy of his brothers who eventually sold him into slavery, touching off a series of events that made little sense apart from God's providence. For the next twenty years, Joseph went from being a servant to a prisoner and then, in a divine twist, to the second in command of all Egypt. Eventually he reunited with his family and from his new position of authority was able to spare them—along with all of Egypt—from the effects of a devastating famine.

After their father died, Joseph's brothers were afraid that he would seek revenge; but instead of returning evil for evil, Joseph freed his brothers by a simple act of forgiveness. A forgiveness that was rooted in his belief in God's providence. He said to them, "Do not fear, for am I in the place of God? As for you, you meant evil against me, but God meant it for good, to bring it about that many people should be kept alive, as they are today."[13]

And with these words, Joseph did not dismiss the reality of how their sin had affected him—he knew all too well the scars from his chains and the weight of false accusations—but he testified to the greater power and greater goodness of God to overcome evil. Because he trusted in God's providence, he was empowered to act, not in response to his brothers' sin, but out of freedom and love.[14]

And it was this same trust in the Father's kind providence that, nearly two thousand years later, led a young Galilean teenager named Mary to say, "Let it be to me according to your word."[15]

Today, with two millennia of hindsight, we understand what a privilege it was for Mary to be chosen to bear the infant Christ. But during those moments when the angel Gabriel came to her and offered such strange words: "You will conceive in your womb

---

13. Genesis 50:19–20.
14. Romans 12:21.
15. Luke 1:38.

and bear a son,"[16] did she understand? And then when the Most High overshadowed her, did she ever wonder, "Why me?" When the whispers started and the knowing glances, when even her fiancé doubted her, did she regret that God has called her to carry His Son? Did she resist the path that He laid before her? We don't read that she did. Instead, Mary used her very body to serve the Lord, testifying to His own steady, intimate love for her. She sings,

> My soul magnifies the Lord,
>   and my spirit rejoices in God my Savior,
> for he has looked on the humble estate
>   of his servant.
> For behold, from now on all
>   generations will call me blessed;
> for he who is mighty has done great
>   things for me,
>   and holy is his name.[17]

When you embrace God's providence in your life, you are free to reflect His power and love. Instead of being paralyzed by what you can't control, you are empowered by the knowledge that God is in control. Instead of being tossed by circumstances and *reacting* to other people's choices, you are empowered to *act* when He calls. You gain control over your own self; and regardless of what may happen, you are free to act out of power and goodness in order to pursue the good of those around you. Just like God providentially pursues yours.

---

16. Luke 1:31.
17. Luke 1:46–49.

Live as You Were Called

*"Two roads diverged in a wood, and I—I took the one less traveled by,
And that has made all the difference."*—Robert Frost

Ultimately, living *imago dei* means embracing whatever path God has laid before you and following when He calls. As Paul advised the Corinthian believers almost two thousand years ago, "Each person [should] lead the life that the Lord has assigned to him, and to which God has called him."[18] And you can only do this by trusting His providence. By fixing your soul on both His power and His love, you will be able to live the life He has given you.

To live not just as if your first breath were ordained, but that every breath after it is as well. To believe that even as each choice presented itself, the hand that offered the choice was His. And to know—despite its twists and curves—He made the road run straight before you and led you exactly where you were meant to go. To know that the *given life*, like all of His gifts, is a good one; and because it is, well, it doesn't much matter why you're not someone else. All that matters is that He has given life to *you*, that He has ordained that *you* would exist, and that He has made *your* life to be beautiful and reflect Him in a unique way. All that matters is that you are precisely who He has made you to be, and one day He will make you to be more than you could ever imagine. One day He will make you like Himself.

---

18. 1 Corinthians 7:17.

part three | *and To Him*

And one day, we too will finally and fully be the image bearers that God has destined us to be. We will finally be able to live in perfect relationship with Him, in harmony with others, and as stewards of His creation. We will finally be glorious as He is glorious.

But it is not a process that we can short-circuit. It is a process that takes a lifetime.

chapter 11

Becoming Real:
Living as a Work in Progress

*"The real Son of God is at your side. He is beginning to
turn you into the same kind of thing as Himself."*
—C. S. Lewis

G. K. Chesterton, that great British philosopher of the
last century, once wrote that he acquired his understanding of the world as a child. "My first and last philosophy,
that which I believe in with unbroken certainty, I learnt in the
nursery . . . a certain way of looking at life, which was created in
me by the fairy tales, but has since been meekly ratified by mere
facts."[1]

If Chesterton is right, it's no surprise that one of the most profound conversations in English literature takes place in a nursery.
In the opening pages of Margery Williams' *The Velveteen Rabbit*,[2]
a splendid new stuffed Rabbit and his toy companion, an older,
wiser, leather horse, talk about what it means to be "Real."

---

1. G. K. Chesterton, *Orthodoxy* (Chicago: 2009 edition by Moody Bible Institute), 76,
77.
2. *The Velveteen Rabbit* by Margery Williams has delighted children and adults since its first
publication in 1922.

"What is REAL?" asked the Rabbit one day, when they were lying side by side near the nursery fender, before Nana came to tidy up the room. "Does it mean having things that buzz inside you and a stick-out handle?"

"Real isn't how you are made," said the Skin Horse. "It's a thing that happens to you. When a child loves you for a long, long time, not just to play with, but REALLY loves you, then you become Real."

"Does it hurt?" asked the Rabbit.

"Sometimes," said the Skin Horse, for he was always truthful. "When you are Real you don't mind being hurt."

"Does it happen all at once, like being wound up," he asked, "or bit by bit?"

"It doesn't happen all at once," said the Skin Horse. "You become. It takes a long time. That's why it doesn't happen often to people who break easily, or have sharp edges, or who have to be carefully kept. Generally, by the time you are Real, most of your hair has been loved off, and your eyes drop out and you get loose in your joints and very shabby. But these things don't matter at all, because once you are Real you can't be ugly, except to people who don't understand . . . but once you are Real you can't become unreal again. It lasts for always."

The Rabbit sighed. He thought it would be a long time before this magic called Real happened to him. He longed to become Real, to know what it felt like; and yet the idea of growing shabby and losing his eyes and whiskers was rather sad. He wished that he could become it without these uncomfortable things happening to him.

Works in Progress

I suspect that most of us feel the same way that little Velveteen Rabbit did. When it comes to finding identity *imago dei*, we long to be Real—to finally be who we were made to be—but that process often takes much longer and hurts much more than we could have ever predicted. Even as we understand that our identity comes from God, even as we begin to pursue relationship with Him and others, even as we submit to the life He has ordained for us, we must still actually *live* that life. We must endure its bumps and scrapes, its joys and sorrows, its victories and defeats.

One of the paradoxes of *imago dei* identity is that we exist in the "in between." We exist in a place that theologian Geerhardus Vos described as the "already" but "not yet." Just as the New Testament describes Christ's kingdom as something that is both present today but not yet fully consummated, we are created in God's image, we share His nature, but we have not fully realized it yet. We have not yet embodied all that we were made to be. We are works in progress.

The apostle Paul captured this tension in Romans when he confesses, "I do not understand my own actions. For I do not do what I want, but I do the very thing I hate . . . I have a desire to do what is right, but not the ability to carry it out. For I do not do the good I want, but the evil I do not want is what I keep doing!" [3]

In these moments, it's easy to become angry with our own foolishness, our inability, our repeated failures and inadequacies, and we give up entirely. We begin to believe that we will never fulfill our purpose, that we will never become who we are meant to be. We want to shut down, hide away, and wait for eternity.

But we must not. Because we are eternal beings, eternity begins today. Eternity is now.

---

3. Romans 7:15, 18–19.

Yet, how do we keep moving forward in the face of such discouragement? How do we keep putting one foot in front of the other as we question whether we are even heading in the right direction? How do we navigate this journey, this journey to become Real?

We navigate it the same way that we started it. We navigate it by embracing what we already are in order to be become what we are destined to be. We navigate it by turning our faces to behold the beauty and wonder of God and embracing His plan to make us like Himself. We navigate it by embracing His faithfulness and reflecting faith in response.

Remember Whose You Are

"If God be for us, who can be against us?"—Paul the apostle

Less than a chapter after Paul confesses his internal struggle—his struggle between what he is and what he longs to be—he reminds us of why we struggle in the first place. We struggle because we are waiting for something. We are waiting "for the glory that is to be revealed." We are waiting to "be set free from bondage . . . and obtain the freedom of the glory of the children of God."[4]

We are waiting to be free. Free to be ourselves. Free to be who we truly are.

For now, though, we must wait in hope and patience. But it is not a hope and patience that we simply conjure up; we can wait in hope and patience because of what God is doing. He has a plan and His love is at work. Paul continues, "For those whom he foreknew he also predestined to be conformed to the image of his Son . . . and those whom he predestined he also called and those

---

4. Romans 8:18–21.

whom he called he also justified and those whom he justified he also glorified."[5]

You can wait in hope and patience because God is actively pursuing your transformation. His love is right now making you who you are meant to be. And it is a love itself so patient and faithful, that "neither death nor life, nor angels nor rulers, nor things present nor things to come, nor powers, nor height nor depth, nor anything else in all creation" can separate us from Him.[6]

Peter teaches this same truth in his second epistle. Peter, that hopeless, helpless wreck of man. Peter, who chided Jesus, who refused to let Him wash his feet, who denied Him in His most vulnerable hour. Who was so broken by his own faithlessness that he went away and wept. This same Peter invites us to take hope in a God who has "called us to his own glory and excellence, by which he has granted to us his precious and very great promises, so that through them you may become partakers of the divine nature."[7]

In other words, your transformation is a sure thing. Your being made like Him *will* happen because He promises it. And so you can trust Him. You can take hope. And because you have hope, you can continue on. You can persevere. You can keep going because this work is His work and He will do it.

Look Back to Look Forward

"Isn't it funny how day by day nothing changes, but when you look back, everything is different."—C. S. Lewis

A couple of years ago, Nathan and I were part of a small group that met together for prayer and fellowship. We often discussed the previous Sunday's sermon, and one evening our group leader

---

5. Romans 8:29–30.
6. Romans 8:38–39.
7. 2 Peter 1:3–4.

asked us to reflect on a comment our pastor had made. He had said something to the effect that our ability to value God's grace was proportional to our ability to feel the weight of our sin. So the question the leader put before us was, "How do you feel about your sinfulness?"

As we began to share, several people mentioned an increasing awareness of their sinfulness—a new ability to feel and experience the weight of their unworthiness—as they matured in Christ. But I was stuck. If I were completely honest, I had to admit that there had been other times in my life that I had felt more burdened by sin than I was presently feeling. But I worried that this would sound "unspiritual." And maybe it was. Maybe I was in a slump and didn't even realize it. Was I taking God's grace for granted? Should I be more broken about the general state of my wretchedness? Did maturing as a Christian mean that I should also mature in the weight of unworthiness I felt?

As I sat there reflecting on the question, still uncertain of my own heart, I realized something. Over the years, Jesus had become more personal, more real to me, and as our fellowship had deepened, I had become more secure in the relationship we shared. I simply did not exist under a cloud of self-loathing as I once had. Why? Because I knew Jesus loves me.

And this love was making me Real.

By living in dependent relationship with Christ, I was becoming more like Him. My heart was changing. And because God was changing me, I found myself less bound by the weight of sin and more often making choices that reflected His nature. But paradoxically, when I do sin, it breaks my heart more deeply. It disturbs me more than it might have before *precisely because I have been changed.* So while I didn't necessarily experience a widespread, pervasive wretchedness, I did experience a deep, piercing brokenness over *specific* sin—times when it felt like my very identity was being torn in two.

It felt that way because it was.

As God transforms you to be more like Him, as your heart mirrors His more perfectly, you can expect two different things: (1) You should experience the ability to increasingly live as you were created to live and (2) You should also feel deeper pain when you do not. And it is this very pain that confirms that you are in the process of changing. This pain helps you remember that you are no longer the person you once were. Even on our worst days, then, even on those days when you feel so out of sorts that you hardly know yourself, you must remember that this discomfort, these growing pains assure that you are made for more.

And this is why you must remember the past even if it is so broken and painful that you'd rather package it up in a box and shove it away in your soul's hall closet. You must remember the past so you can rejoice in who God is making you to be. Because as dangerous as it is to presume upon God's goodness and continue to live in your old identity, it is equally dangerous to overlook the work He has already accomplished and is accomplishing in you.

When you do look back and you can actually see God transforming you, bit by bit, ever so steadily, you can have hope. You can remember that this is His work and that what He starts, He will finish. You remember that because He has *begun* a good work in you, He must complete it.[8] And amazingly this faithfulness— God's persistent, steady faithfulness—engenders our own faithfulness in response. When we remember all that He has been for us, it strengthens our faith in Him and our resolve to continue to find our true selves in Him. When we turn to behold His faithfulness, we end up reflecting it in our own lives.

---

8. Philippians 1:6.

Lives of Faithfulness

"To progress is always to begin again." —Martin Luther

Several years ago, I worked in the expatriate business community helping newly relocated businesspeople navigate the complexities of American culture and the English language. One day, I met a woman who would become one of my dearest friends, despite the fact that we had very little in common. Michal is fifteen years my senior, a native of Israel, and by her own confession a religious agnostic at best. She is an exotic beauty with straight, black hair; a smooth olive complexion; and smart, vibrant eyes.

Michal married Eli (not their real names) when they were both in their early twenties. Over the course of the next several decades, they navigated multiple career changes, postgrad work, the birth of their three daughters, and overseas work assignments, and they eventually immigrated to Canada where they started life all over again. In a day when divorce rates are astronomically high, any one of these situations could have ended their marriage. But none did, and this struck me. Michal and I were talking about this one day when she told me her secret.

"Hannah," she said, "I have been married four times."

I was shocked. Was there more to my friend than I knew?

But then she continued, "I have been married four times— each time to the same man."

Michal went on to explain that the key to their long marriage was choosing each other over and over again. Through all the cycles of change, through each period of personal growth, even through the times they found themselves drifting apart, they survived by continuing to come back to each other. They kept choosing each other.

This is the essence of faithfulness. This is what it means to persevere.

And finding identity as image bearers happens the same way. As God proves Himself faithful to us, as He perseveres in His love for us, we respond by waking up each day to again find our sense of self in Him. Each day, we turn our faces to Him in order to image His nature. Each day, we turn ourselves over to His love and His power. Each day, we choose Him again. And even when we fail to do this, when we drift, He does not. He remains faithful. He remains our constant star, our True North, our all in all.

In many ways, becoming Real—becoming who He created us to be—is not so much a single event as a way of living, a way of existing. It is not simply a wedding; it is a marriage. Even in those moments when you've stepped from the path, when you feel like you've lost yourself, finding yourself is as simple as turning back to Him. Finding yourself means returning to "the Shepherd . . . of your soul."[9] Finding yourself means doing this over and over and over again until you finally become who you already are.

Growing Up into Christ

I became a mother on a rainy July afternoon when our daughter made her entrance into this world a week later than we'd expected. Like any first-time parent, I felt overwhelmed and in awe of this new person I cradled in my arms. Holding her felt like holding the world. Her deep, brown eyes peeked out at me from behind the folds of a pink-and-blue striped blanket, and I couldn't help but marvel at the sheer possibility bound up her in 7 pound, 6 ounce, 19 ½-inch body. All that she would ever be—all her gifts, all her hopes, all her aspirations—were, in some way, already present in those first moments of her life, embodied within her as a seed embodies the potential of a future plant.

---

9. 1 Peter 2:25.

Over the years, I've realized that one of the greatest joys of parenting is having a front-row seat to watch as my children become who God has made them to be. With each first step, each lisping syllable, each loose tooth, I learn a bit more about who they already are. It's like watching a bud slowly open or hearing a secret be revealed. And it is this very process—this shared life—that binds my heart to theirs.

It is this shared life that makes me more their mother than simple biology ever could.

I can't help but believe that it is the same with our relationship with God. Does the process of change *itself* enable us to live *imago dei*? Does the process *itself* bind us to Him in a way that an instant transformation would not? As He celebrates our first faltering steps and our lisping, babbling praise, as He rescues us when we fall and feeds us our daily bread, as we continue to turn our faces toward Him, we find ourselves increasingly bound to Him. We find ourselves in the middle of the very relationship that makes us the image bearers we are meant to be.

Thus through this shared life, we "are being transformed into the same image from one degree of glory to another."[10] We are finally growing up to be who we've always been meant to be. We are finally becoming "mature, attaining to the whole measure of the fullness of Christ."[11]

Becoming Real

At the end of *The Velveteen Rabbit*, our little hero finds himself relegated to the garbage heap because his Boy had contracted scarlet fever and all his toys must be burned. He is broken, worn, and

---

10. 2 Corinthians 3:18.
11. Ephesians 4:13–15 (NIV).

alone. Lying there he wonders, "Of what use was it to be loved and lose one's beauty and become Real if it all ended like this?"

> And a tear, a real tear, trickled down his little shabby velvet nose and fell to the ground. And then a strange thing happened. For where the tear had fallen a flower grew out of the ground . . . and presently the blossom opened, and out of it there stepped a fairy.

> "I am the nursery magic Fairy," she said. "I take care of all the playthings that the children have loved. When they are old and worn out. . . then I come and take them away with me and turn them into Real."

> "Wasn't I Real before?" asked the little Rabbit.

> "You were Real to the Boy," the Fairy said, "because he loved you. Now you shall be Real to every one."

And one day, we too will finally and fully be Real—we will finally be the image bearers that God has destined us to be. We will finally be able to live in perfect relationship with Him, in harmony with others, and as stewards of His creation. We will finally be glorious as He is glorious.

But it is not a process that we can short-circuit. It is a process that takes a lifetime. And it is a process that often involves both more pain and more joy than we could ever anticipate. But even in the waiting, even in the longing, even in the "groaning . . . for redemption,"[12] God's faithful love is at work. This is Christ being formed within you; this is the hope of glory.[13]

---

12. Romans 8:22–23.
13. Galatians 4:19; Colossians 1:27.

chapter 12

Hope of Glory:
Eternal Life in the Here and Now

"I saw Eternity the other night,
Like a great ring of pure and endless light,
All calm, as it was bright." —Henry Vaughan

A couple of summers ago, I was invited to a friend's wedding in the city where we had been students together ten years earlier. My husband couldn't get away to accompany me, so my daughter and I took our first road trip. My eighty-three-year-old grandmother happened to live in that same city, so the Sunday after the wedding, I arranged to pick her up for church and lunch afterward.

We arrived at church with plenty of time for her to get settled and for me to reminisce. This was, after all, the church where two years earlier we had said our final goodbyes to my grandfather who was the family patriarch in every sense of the word. This was also the church I had attended through college. The one where Nathan first decided to ask me out after spotting me at a service. The one that had been so central to our early relationship that I sometimes wonder if we would have continued dating were it not for those Sundays when we found ourselves squished together in the middle of a pew of college students.

So there I was, over a decade later with a seven-year-old daughter on one side and an aging grandmother on the other.

The text for the morning was 1 Peter 4:12–19, and the sermon was entitled, "Sharing in Christ's Suffering." A few minutes into the message, the pastor observed that suffering was part of Christ's call to His disciples from the beginning. He had warned them about it but had also assured them that their suffering would ultimately be worthwhile. "But," the pastor continued, "the Lord also taught His disciples that it would be wrong—shortsighted—to attempt to calculate the reward based on this life alone. For the fullest and most accurate assessment, they would also need eternity."[1]

I don't know if it was his words, my propensity to daydream, or simply the layering of the years and all the memories connected to that sanctuary piling up on top of each other, but as I listened I had a kind of awakening, a realization that my life couldn't be reduced to this moment. My identity stretched from the day I was born through the span of my life and on into eternity.

In one sense, it could seem that the college girl I was ten years earlier was not the same woman sitting in the pew that day; and who I was that day is not who I am now or who I will be tomorrow. But in another sense, I most certainly am the same person. Whether it was ten years in the past or ten years in the future, I have always been and will always be me. I haven't always been the best me; I haven't always been the me who I was created to be; and I hope in the future to be more that than I am now; but I am still one person. I am still me.

The truth about *imago dei* identity is that we really cannot measure the scope of our lives; we cannot fully understand ourselves by this present moment alone. Discovering who God has made us to

---

1. Sermon by Pastor Robert Vincent preached on July 22, 2012, at Mt. Calvary Baptist Church, Greenville, South Carolina.

be requires both this life and the life to come. This "timelessness" of identity is the direct result of being made in His image, of being made in the image of a God who Himself exists outside of time. Because God is eternal, we are destined for eternal life as well.

Seasons of Life

"What day is it?"
"It's today," squeaked Piglet.
"My favorite day," said Pooh.
—A. A. Milne

But even as we are destined for eternal life, we get there through time. We live life through individual moments. And the beauty, the wisdom of this, is that God uses these moments to bring us into union with His own eternality. He uses time to make us the eternal image bearers we are meant to be.

Solomon wrestles with this paradox in Ecclesiastes 3, which is perhaps one of the best known passages of Scripture even among those who don't claim to be in any way religious. The passage opens with Solomon's celebrated words about the cycles of time:

For everything there is a season, and a time for every matter under heaven:

a time to be born, and a time to die;
a time to plant, and a time to pluck up what is planted;
a time to kill, and a time to heal;
a time to break down, and a time to build up;
a time to weep, and a time to laugh;
a time to mourn, and a time to dance;
a time to cast away stones, and a time to gather stones together;
a time to embrace, and a time to refrain from embracing;
a time to seek, and a time to lose;

a time to keep, and a time to cast away;

a time to tear, and a time to sew;

a time to keep silence, and a time to speak;

a time to love, and a time to hate;

a time for war, and a time for peace.

These words resonate with preacher and pop star alike because they capture something we all know to be true about reality. Despite our desire to control life, despite our desire to slow down the clock, time continues to "turn, turn, turn."[2]

Some people deal with this instability by adopting a "let it be" attitude; they simply submit themselves to the inevitability of change and say things like "Death is part of living" or "It's all part of the circle of life." Others deal with it by determining to *carpe diem*, to pack their lives full of experiences, to live every moment as if it were their last. But even as they grasp each moment, the grains of time still slip through their fingers.

As much as Solomon is affirming the natural cycle of life, he has a greater point to make. And it's a point that many people miss because, as famous as these first verses are, the ones that follow aren't equally so. Immediately after this poem, Solomon writes about God's eternality. He writes that although our lives are constantly changing, "whatever God does endures forever; nothing can be added to it, nor anything taken from it . . . that which is, already has been; that which is to be, already has been."[3]

Solomon's point is this: because life is so unpredictable, because it cycles through various seasons without warning, we must fix our hope on a God who does not. We must find identity in the one thing that remains the same. We must find identity in the Great I Am.

---

2. Pete Seeger used this same passage of Scripture for The Byrds' 1962 chart-topping hit, "Turn! Turn! Turn!"
3. Ecclesiastes 3:14–15.

Throughout Scripture, God identifies Himself as the "I Am"—the Ancient of Days, the Alpha and Omega, the Beginning and the End. In Psalm 90:2, Moses describes Him as "everlasting to everlasting." Before the world began, He was.[4] And even when He did confine Himself to time, when He entered our reality in the form of Jesus, He declared, "Before Abraham was, I Am."

As His Image bearers, we can be content with nothing less. We are timeless beings who share the timeless nature of our God. As Solomon writes in this very passage, He "has put eternity in [our] hearts." And the beauty of this is that the cycles of life actually propel us toward Him because in the midst of constant change, our souls long for the Unchangeable. We long for Him.

And suddenly everything comes full circle.

Because once we turn to embrace Him, once we find our stability in His eternal identity instead of the pages of the calendar, we are free to enter whatever new cycle He brings. We are freed from longing for the past and regret over our failures and can look back on those days with gratitude and peace. We are freed from anxiety and impatience about the future and can look forward to it with joy and expectation. We can embrace the seasons of life as God-ordained and live fully in each, hallowing it as a sacred gift. Solomon concludes this passage by writing that "there is nothing better for them than to be joyful and to do good as long as they live; also that everyone should eat and drink and take pleasure in all his toil—this is God's gift to man."

Time becomes less of a thief and more of a servant. Even as your days and years fly quickly by, even as the vapor of your life curls and dances upward, you can have confidence that the God who made time is the same God who makes all things beautiful in His time. And when you are here, you can finally begin to experience a bit of the timelessness for which you were created.

---

4. Ephesians 1:4.

Crossing Jordan

"The Jordan River is chilly and cold,
It chills the body but not the soul." —Negro spiritual

In the final pages of John Bunyan's classic, *The Pilgrim's Progress*, Christian and his companion Hopeful reach a point where they can finally see the object of their journey, the Celestial City. Bunyan writes that "the reflection of the Sun upon the City (for the City was pure gold) was so extremely glorious, that they could not as yet with open face behold it." But between the two pilgrims and the City lies a swollen, raging river with no bridge and no means to cross over. When Christian sees this, he begins to despair and look for a way around it; but there is none.

Eventually they enter the River, and Bunyan writes that, mystically, they "find it deeper or shallower, as [they] believe in the King of the Place." Hopeful quickly finds his footing and encourages Christian that he can feel the bottom. But Christian begins to sink, struggling in the water, flailing, gasping, drowning. He thinks of his past, his brokenness, his faithlessness, and begins to fear that the River will snatch him away and he will never enter the City.

Hopeful, seeing his friend struggle, encourages him to press forward, but his words have no effect until he says, "Be of good cheer, Jesus Christ maketh thee whole!"

And with that Christian brake out with a loud voice, Oh I see him again! And he tells me, When thou passest through the Waters, I will be with thee; and through the Rivers, they shall not overflow thee.[5] Then they both took courage, and the Enemy was after that as still as a stone.

5. Isaiah 43:2.

The River, of course, represents Death, that last, great enemy. And if I'm honest, I know that I am more like Christian than Hopeful, and I don't think I'm alone in this. In fact, this aversion to death is fundamental to *imago dei* identity because as image bearers, we were created to be eternal. Remember that those first image bearers ate from the Tree of *Life* before they were expelled from Eden. In Revelation 22, John foresees the same Tree of Life flourishing in Paradise. Death is unnatural for us; we were never intended to die but to share in God's own life. Because of this, we come factory set to avoid death at all cost.

This shows itself in both great and small ways. If you think about it, a midlife crisis is nothing more than a person searching for identity in the face of her own mortality. It isn't so much about mid-*life* as it is about death; she is panicking because she realizes that her life on this earth is half over. Death has never been closer than it is today. Than it is this very moment.

This is also why the antiaging industry, with its promises to do everything from restore a youthful libido to reduce fine lines, has become a multibillion-dollar enterprise. Go to any given drugstore and you'll find shelves and shelves of products devoted to turning back the clock. And the more expensive it is, the more likely it is to be locked in a plastic case or have a security device attached. (Whenever I see this, I can't help but conjure up an image of a desperate woman looking over her shoulder as she surreptitiously slips a vial of Oil of Olay into her oversized quilted handbag.) The truth is we are afraid to age because we are afraid to die, and aging is a constant reminder of our certain end.

But as natural as it is to want to avoid death, the *fear* of death can actually become debilitating, locking us into a prison of anxiety and desperation. Hebrews teaches that Satan even uses our fear as a weapon to "subject [us] to lifelong slavery."[6] Death hangs

6. Hebrews 2:15.

over us, with its sinister shadows, telling us that there is nothing more powerful, nothing more fearful, nothing more final. Death tells us that there is simply nothing more. And we quiver and quake under its spell and will do anything to escape.

But like Satan's other slanders, this too is a lie. The truth is that there is nothing more powerful than the One who is all in all. There is nothing more powerful than the One who first breathed life into these earthly bodies. There is nothing more powerful than the One from whom and through whom and to whom flow all things.

And even death itself cannot separate us from His love.[7]

Because of His strong love, Jesus Christ—"eternally begotten of the Father, God from God, light from light"[8]—came to conquer death. When He died, He died for us. When He rose again three days later, He destroyed death's power over us as well.[9] And from His own eternal, abundant life, He offers life to us today.

Like Christian and Hopeful, we can pass through death but not feel its sting or taste its bitterness. Death has no power over those who "believe in the King of the Place." Death has no power over those who hide in the One who is Eternal Life Himself. And it is by this great eternal power that He can take the greatest threat to your identity and make it the very means by which you finally become the image bearer you are meant to be. By His great eternal power, He takes death itself and makes it a gateway to glory.

Eternal Glory

When Christian and Hopeful come out of the River, Bunyan writes that they leave "their mortal Garments behind them" in exchange for the "white Robes" of the City. Bunyan is illustrating

---

7. Romans 8:37–39.
8. The Nicene Creed, written AD 325.
9. Hebrews 2:14–15.

what Paul teaches in 1 Corinthians when he says that "this perishable body must put on the imperishable, and this mortal body must put on immortality."[10] When we pass through death, we experience a fundamental change in our identity. Just as through birth, "we have borne the image of the man of dust," through death, "we shall also bear the image of the man of heaven."[11]

When we think of "eternal life," we often understand it as simply the lengthening of the life we now have; but Scripture speaks of it in a different way. In a much more radical, startling, and—dare I say it—*real* way. When Scripture speaks of "eternal life," it is more than an extension of our earthly experience; it is a fundamental transformation of life itself. It is a new kind of living, a living like we've never before known.

Eternal life means entering into the life of God Himself.

Shortly before His death, Jesus asked the Father to glorify Him so He could give eternal life to His followers. He then explained what that means: "And this is eternal life, that they know you the only true God, and Jesus Christ whom you have sent."[12] Jesus is not stealing away the physical dimension of "eternal life"; He is broadening it. He is articulating the same truth that Paul does when he says that eternal life is both "glory and honor *and* immortality."[13] To know God, to live in communion with Him, has far more reaching effects than simply extending our physical life. It means finally sharing in His nature in a way that we cannot now imagine; and as a result, becoming who we were created to be—becoming ourselves—by becoming image bearers who perfectly reflect the majesty of our God.

God, who pulses and radiates throughout with glory. God,

---

10. 1 Corinthians 15:53.
11. 1 Corinthians 15:49.
12. John 17:3.
13. Romans 2:7.

who is so brilliant that Moses had to veil his face after looking on Him. God, who is so abundantly life-giving that death itself could not keep Him in the grave. To know this God and His Son, Jesus Christ, is no metaphysical consolation prize. To know this God, to finally join in perfect union and complete harmony with His nature, this is eternal life.

And when we finally see Him—when death carries us to His side or He returns in the glory of the skies—we shall be like Him. And in that moment, we will be swallowed up—not by death, but by *life*.[14] Swallowed up into the ever-brilliant, ever-pulsing, ever-giving, ever-loving Life of God Himself. Because while we may be content to experience life as we know it, God wants us to experience life as He knows it.

It's hard for us to imagine, to think about what this means. We have no way to understand the glory that we will exist in—the glory that will exist in us—other than by turning to behold God's own glory. Second Corinthians 4:17–18 says that this "eternal weight of glory [is] beyond all comparison"; in order to understand it we must look not "to the things that are seen but to the things that are unseen." But even as we do, we realize that we are unable to bear it. Like Moses, we must hide our faces, incapable of looking at the eternal, everlasting nature of our God. We stand in awe of His love that never ends, His grace so freely bestowed, His wisdom that uses the foolishness of men to praise Him.

This is a mystery, but it has been His plan from eternity. It has been His plan to make us like Himself. It has been His plan to bring us to glory. In a moment, in the twinkling of an eye, we shall be changed.[15] And in that moment, the facets of your identity will finally align and His nature will radiate through you, bursting

---

14. 2 Corinthians 5:4.
15. 1 Corinthians 15:51–52.

forth in glorious splendor. As C. S. Lewis writes:[16]

> He will make the feeblest and filthiest of us into a god or god-
> dess,[17] a dazzling, radiant, immortal creature, pulsating all
> through with such energy and joy and wisdom and love as we
> cannot now imagine, a bright stainless mirror which reflects back
> to God perfectly (though, of course, on a smaller scale) His own
> boundless power and delight and goodness.

And finally, finally, we will be like Him.

Even So Come

"It was fitting that he, for whom and by whom all things exist,
[bring] many sons to glory." —*Hebrews 2:10*

This book began with the question, "Who am I and why am I here?"
And while it will take a lifetime to uncover it, the answer is fundamentally a simply one. You are an image bearer of your great and glorious God. You were created to reflect and represent Him through
your life. This means that your identity is found in His identity; and
you will never know yourself, never be yourself, apart from Him.

It also means embracing the hard truth that most of the time we
do not look to Him to understand ourselves. Most of the time, we
look to other people and other things. And when we do, we come
desperately short of the glory that God intends for us. But when
we repent of this, when we turn back to Him in the person of Jesus

---

16. C. S. Lewis, *Mere Christianity* (Nashville, TN: Broadman and Holman Publishers, 1996), 176.

17. Lewis is not referring to pagan gods and goddesses of demonic origins but to people as *imago dei* representations of the One True God. Asaph uses similar language in Psalm 82:6 when he says, "You are gods, sons of the Most High, all of you." And Jesus Him-self quotes this passage in John 10:34.

Christ—the Image become perfect Image Bearer—He promises to make us who we are meant to be. He promises to make us new.

Near the end of Revelation, John is granted a vision of eternal life. He writes,

> And I heard a loud voice from the throne saying, "Behold, the dwelling place of God is with man. He will dwell with them, and they will be his people, and God himself will be with them as their God. He will wipe away every tear from their eyes, and death shall be no more, neither shall there be mourning, nor crying, nor pain anymore, for the former things have passed away." And he who was seated on the throne said, "Behold, I am making all things new. . . . I am the Alpha and the Omega, the beginning and the end."

Our God is making all things new. He is making you new. And He can do this for the fundamental reason that all things flow "from Him and through Him and to Him." Including us. Especially us.

One day, when He appears, you also will appear with Him in glory. One day, He will transform your lowly body to be like His glorious body. One day, you will shine "like the brightness of the sky above . . . and like the stars forever."[18] And one day—oh, glorious day—you will be like Him because you will see Him as He is.

Even so, come, Lord Jesus.

Quickly come.

---

18. Daniel 12:3.

STRIPPED

978-0-8024-0965-2

Stripped is about understanding the stripping process that must take place for sold out Christians to be used by God to build His kingdom. It is about the surrendered and broken Christian life, the life that God uses to accomplish His purposes through every one of His followers.

Also available as an ebook

MOODY
Publishers™

From the Word to Life
www.MoodyPublishers.com

UNITED

United will explore the importance of pursuing diversity in the church by sharing the author's unique experiences growing up in the south and attending a predominately white church. She champions the theology of diversity throughout the book through the Scriptures providing compelling reasons to pursue diversity. Trillia will also weave in story describing her friendship with two women of different ethnicities.

978-0-8024-1014-6

Also available as an ebook

MOODY
Publishers™

From the Word to Life
www.MoodyPublishers.com